SPIRITUAL AWAKENING

by
Darshan Singh

SAWAN KIRPAL PUBLICATIONS

Library of Congress Catalog Card Number: 81-50726
ISBN 0-918224-11-X

First Edition: 1982
Second Printing: 1983
Third Printing: 1986

Published by Sawan Kirpal Publications,
Bowling Green, Virginia 22427, and
2 Canal Road, Vijay Nagar, Delhi-110009, India

Printed in the United States of America

I OFFER THESE SPONTANEOUS NOTES
TO
HAZUR BABA SAWAN SINGH JI MAHARAJ
AND
PARAM SANT KIRPAL SINGH JI MAHARAJ
AT WHOSE LOTUS FEET
I EXPERIENCED THE PANGS AND ECSTASY
OF
DIVINE LOVE
FOR
IT IS THEIR CELESTIAL MUSIC
WHICH FLOWS THROUGH
THIS HUMBLE REED.

ABOUT THE AUTHOR

Darshan Singh is the founder of Sawan Kirpal Ruhani Mission, a spiritual organization with international headquarters in Delhi, India, and over three hundred centers throughout the world. He is currently the president of the World Fellowship of Religions, and of the World Unity of Man Society. In addition, he is acclaimed as India's greatest living mystic poet writing in the Urdu language, and one of his collections of poems, *Manzil-e-Noor* (*Abode of Light*), won for him the Urdu Academy Award for poetry. His English publications include: *The Secret of Secrets*, spiritual talks; and *Cry of the Soul*, mystic poetry. He has also published hundreds of articles and poems on spiritual topics in various periodicals.

Born in 1921, he began his spiritual training under the guidance of his father, Sant Kirpal Singh, who was the founder of Ruhani Satsang, the first president of the World Fellowship of Religions, the organizer of the first World Unity of Man Conference, and the author of over twenty books on spirituality. Darshan Singh was initiated into the spiritual science in 1926 by Baba Sawan Singh of Beas, and he served in various capacities in the missions of his Master and his Master's successor, Sant Kirpal Singh. In 1942 he began work as a civil servant and rose to a high position in the Indian government. In 1974, before his physical departure from earth, Sant Kirpal Singh chose Darshan Singh as his spiritual successor.

SANT DARSHAN SINGH

BABA SAWAN SINGH
(1858-1948)

SANT KIRPAL SINGH
(1894-1974)

PREFACE

The Golden Age begins with each of us—it begins *within* each of us. There is a sure, definite path which we can follow to realize the totality of our potential— the path of Spiritual Awakening. It is at once man's oldest and his newest preoccupation. We need only look at recent medical research in life-after-death experiences, and studies in the New Physics, to realize that science itself is now confirming the insights of the ancient prophets and mystics. The language and symbols may change as time passes, or as we move from one culture to another, but the underlying truth is the same.

The talks collected here fall into three parts. Part I, "Eternal Science," deals with the fundamentals of spirituality. Part II, "Crucible," examines the daily discipline necessary for success on the spiritual path. Part III, "Alchemy of Love," considers love as that alchemy which alone transforms the human into the divine. Finally, Part IV comprises questions and answers which explore related issues.

If some of the chapter titles appear to be unusual for a collection on mysticism and spirituality, there is an unusual explanation. I made my first tour of America during the summer of 1978. A two-month program of lectures was planned, but much to the dismay of those traveling with me, the suitcase filled with all my notes, articles, and manuscripts—the material for my lectures—was lost by the airlines! With talks scheduled for almost every night, what was to be done? As I then remarked, "The choice is to turn and flee, or to plunge headlong into the program." Relying on the grace of the great Masters, Hazur Baba Sawan Singh and Sant Kirpal Singh, I decided to take the plunge. According to an old tradition in India, parents are honor-bound to preserve the purity of their daughter up to the time they give her away in marriage. So I prayed to the Masters to preserve their own honor, and they came to my rescue.

Because of these circumstances, the themes of the talks often suggested themselves by the accidents of the moment. On one occasion, as I walked to a hotel lecture-hall a marriage party was in progress, and the result was "Eternal Spouse" [pp. 85-91]. On another, the hotel's air-conditioning failed, and the guests squirmed in discomfort. This mechanical breakdown became my point of departure for "Air-conditioning" [pp. 158-161]. This collection of talks also includes several delivered in India, and these too follow a similar pattern of development. After particularly heavy rains, floods destroyed much property and tragically took the lives of many people in Delhi. Witnessing the extent of this disaster on the way to deliver a weekly discourse, I spoke of the "Boat of Naam" [pp. 40-48].

I am indebted to Vinod Sena, Ruth Seader, and Jay and Ricki Linksman for preparing this volume for publication. Some of the chapters contained herein have previously appeared in periodicals, and I am grateful to Malcolm and Kate Tillis for reviewing those chapters. Thanks are also due to those who assisted in transcribing, typing, typesetting, paste-up, or proofreading. They are Jamie and Martha Smith, John and Isabel Wolf, George Barham, Ron and Valerie Tarrant, Sandy Glassman, Dale and Marsha McCurley, Alex Vafiadis, John Servidio, Jonathan and Douglas Kruger, Chris and Katie McCluney, Jane Disinger, Georg Koester, Meena Kumari, Joanne Wiemeyer, Mary Paton, Eliot Rosen, Ed Wallace, Julius Burt, Bruce Dodd, and Sham and Sunaina Bhatia.

—Darshan Singh

CONTENTS

PREFACE   xi

PART I
ETERNAL SCIENCE

One   SPIRITUAL AWAKENING   3
Two   CONQUERING DEATH   8
Three   SHORTCUTS TO
             SPIRITUALITY   20
Four   PERFECT SCIENTIST   32
Five   BOAT OF NAAM   40
Six   THE SAINT AND THE
             SCHOLAR   49
Seven   SCIENCE OF INNER
             RELAXATION   62
Eight   BIRTHDAY BEYOND TIME
             AND SPACE   69
Nine   FINAL CHAPTER OF
             TRANSMIGRATION   78
Ten   ETERNAL SPOUSE   85
Eleven   PREDICAMENT OF MAN   92
Twelve   PREDICAMENT OF GOD   100

PART II
CRUCIBLE

Thirteen   DIVINE BEAUTICIAN   113
Fourteen   THE MIRROR   118
Fifteen   MESSAGE OF FALL   123
Sixteen   TRUE COLORS   129
Seventeen NEW DEFINITIONS OF LOVE   135

Eighteen	VEIL OF EGO	140
Nineteen	VEGETARIAN DIET	149
Twenty	AIR-CONDITIONING	158
Twenty-One	PARENTS AND CHILDREN	162

PART III
ALCHEMY OF LOVE

Twenty-Two	WAITING FOR THE BELOVED	177
Twenty-Three	PANGS OF LOVE	186
Twenty-Four	TWO TYPES OF LOVE	194
Twenty-Five	RUNNING COMMENTARY OF THE MIND	201
Twenty-Six	GIVING AND RECEIVING	213
Twenty-Seven	NINE SIGNS OF A LOVER	219
Twenty-Eight	CONTINUOUS STRUGGLE	229
Twenty-Nine	SURRENDER	234

PART IV
QUESTIONS AND ANSWERS

Thirty	NEED FOR A LIVING MASTER	249
Thirty-One	INITIATION	263
Thirty-Two	DEATH AND KARMA	268
Thirty-Three	POSITIVE MYSTICISM	280
Thirty-Four	LOVE AND DEVOTION	303

PART I

ETERNAL
SCIENCE

CHAPTER ONE
SPIRITUAL AWAKENING

Mankind has always dreamed of a Golden Age. Some imagine it as having existed in the remote past, while others project it into a distant future. For those who have the eyes to read the signs, the Golden Age of spirituality has already begun, and we are witnessing its dawn. Already, young and old throughout the world are beginning to seek spiritual awakening.

People today are realizing as never before the ephemeral nature of material life. Although we have made great strides in science and technology, we find humanity is no closer to happiness. The world is still strife-torn, the crime rate is ever-increasing, wars continue to be fought between people of one religion and another, between people of one color and another, between one country and another. Even within the family there is unhappiness. Family life has deteriorated, and every day I come across cases of broken homes, uncared-for children, and forsaken elderly parents. When I inquire from the young who come to me, "How are your parents?" I am often told,

"I do not know—my parents divorced when I was a child and since then my parents remarried more than once. Now I do not have much contact with my father or my mother." Parents tell me that their children are not respectful or obedient. And when the elderly come to me they say they are uncared-for and forgotten, and may even have been placed in old-age homes.

Not only family life, but community life is also vanishing. There is such an emphasis on individuality that we are not concerned about our neighbors. A man may fall seriously ill and need help—even die—and those living next door may not learn of it for weeks.

With our material advances we have been able to acquire so many luxuries, but we have not been able to bring peace to the world, to our countries, to our communities, to our families, or to our own souls. We may build the tallest building in the world, possess the costliest diamond, become president of the richest nation, and fulfill all our sensuous cravings, but such achievements, we find to our dismay, do not give us lasting peace and happiness. We then begin to ask, "Can we not seek something which will give us permanent happiness and bliss?"

This quest is leading us to explore numerous paths and movements which promise peace to the soul. In this age of spiritual awakening we find people returning to more healthy ways of living: vegetarian and natural diets, physical exercises, hatha yoga, natural remedies for disease, wellness and fitness programs, and abstinence from smoking, drinking and intoxicating drugs which harm the body. Others who long for world peace join organizations to further that end: Ecological groups, organizations to deal with world hunger, social welfare societies, world peace organizations and human rights movements are a few examples. Others are trying to raise the moral and ethical values of mankind, especially in the fields of politics, education and business.

More and more people are turning to spiritual paths. Meditation is no longer something obscure; it is being practiced by people of all religions, ages and avocations. These people are joining different groups and are practicing various forms of yoga, Transcendental Meditation, Zen Buddhism, Sufism, and the like. Some forms of meditation are becoming a daily feature in the lives of doctors, educators, scientists, lawyers, businessmen, politicians, those in the creative arts and all other walks of life. Meditation is now being recognized as a means to relieve depression and reduce the tensions of daily life. It is being used by many to increase productivity on the job, to help the concentration of students who have learning difficulties, and to give those who were addicted to drugs a natural means to overcome their problems. While many practice meditation to relieve anxiety and become more productive, a growing number of serious seekers are turning to meditation to solve the mystery of life and death.

All our lives we are learning, and in a sense always remain students. When we are children we learn from our parents and teachers, later we learn from our college professors, and even when we take up our professions we learn from those who are already proficient in that field. In spite of all the books we have in our libraries, when we wish to master a subject, we go to living teachers. If this is the case with outer knowledge, how much more important it is to have the help of an adept when it comes to inner knowledge. In the past, esoteric knowledge was confined to the lucky few who were disciples of the great Masters of their time. But in the age of spiritual awakening, such knowledge is available to everyone. This is a significant step in the spiritual evolution of man. If today we see spirituality as the universal core of religion, no longer tied to rituals and dogmas, no longer the preserve of priests and theologians, it is because of saints such as Baba Sawan Singh (1858-1948) and Sant Kirpal Singh (1894-1974). These great Masters at whose feet I had the privilege of learning, presented spirituality as the most perfect science—the science of the soul. Spirituality is a practical discipline in which, under the guidance of a competent teacher, we can transcend the body and know for ourselves that we are spirit. It is the most natural path, one that does not require us to leave our family, job, home or religion. Like God's other gifts, it is free and available to all.

Many people fear that the Golden Age will be preceded by a world catastrophe and cataclysmic upheavels. It has been said that whenever there is a change from one age to the other, it is accompanied by a dissolution or grand dissolution. But as Sant Kirpal Singh said, the Golden Age will not be ushered in by worldwide destruction. The new age will come about through a change of hearts. When the day dawns, the night seems to linger and there are many shades of gray before the sun comes into its full glory. Likewise, there are many stages before the new consciousness comes into its own and bathes the world in spiritual light.

As more and more people take to meditation and learn to transcend their limited physical consciousness, they will begin to see that all are children of the same Father, of the One God. The walls which separate man from man will gradually crumble and we will create a world in which every individual—no matter how humble—is respected and cared for.

We are witnessing the dawn of a spiritual revolution. By definition, such a revolution, unlike political, social or economic ones, cannot be enforced from without. It is an inner revolution which centers on a change of consciousness. We cannot convert others, we can only convert ourselves. If we can accomplish this transformation we will not only hasten the spiritual dawn, but will ourselves bask in its full glory.

CHAPTER TWO
CONQUERING DEATH

The coming of the Golden Age was announced by Sant Kirpal Singh in 1974 at the World Conference on the Unity of Man, and indeed there is a growing spiritual awakening all over the world. Evidence of this can be seen in the increasing interest in solving the mystery of life and death. Throughout history, people have been ignorant about death and have tried to avoid facing its inevitability. I remember when I was in college, it was not considered polite to talk about death. Whenever we talked of death, our elders would brush us aside saying, "Talk of something else, talk of something better." I find the condition in the West no different than in India. For example, a recent survey by psychologists shows that in America most adults cannot remember even one instance in childhood when death was discussed in the family. If it was at all discussed, it was with great discomfort. For the past one or two generations, the young seldom got to see anybody dying. Generally in America, the old do not live with the young. Whenever anyone is terminally ill, he is sent to a hospital or an old-age home where nobody can see him writhing in pain, and he dies unseen and unsung.

But now people are beginning to face the fact of man's mortality, and are even coming to realize that we continue to live after we die. Recently, many books have been published in Europe and America concerning life after death. Dr. Raymond Moody's *Life After Life* was one of the earliest and most popular. Moody describes in his book the experiences of a number of people who were declared clinically dead, but who revived, and related the experiences they underwent during the period in which they were declared to have been dead. Almost all of them experienced hearing various sounds and seeing flashes of light. Some met a benevolent, radiant form who helped them examine their deeds in life. This book created a sensation in the West, but it has not come as a big surprise to those in the East. The Western world is now becoming aware of what was said hundreds of years ago in the Sikh scriptures and thousands of years ago in the ancient Indian scriptures. It is only now that science has begun to touch the threshold of the realms which have been familiar to the saints since the dawn of creation.

In Indian literature written thousands of years ago we find mention of a devoted wife named Savitri. Because of her purity and great devotion, at her husband's death she was able to see Yama, the Angel of Death, who had come to take the soul of her spouse. She was able to transcend her physical body and follow the Angel of Death until she persuaded him to return the soul of her husband to human life. Then her husband, having been physically dead, returned to his body for a second lease on life.

We also find many references to death in the writings of the Greeks. Plato said that life is an impediment for our soul, and our soul could be liberated upon our death.

There has been an inherent desire for immortality in man since the dawn of history. If we study Egyptian civilization of about five thousand years ago we find they had perfected the technique of embalming in the hope that the kings, queens and princes who died would come back to life again. When the rulers died, their ministers and pages were put to death and embalmed along with their masters. In this way, when the royalty came to life they would immediately be attended upon by their pages and ministers.

Man has also sought to fulfill the desire for immortality through the fine arts. Shah Jahan, the great Moghul emperor, sought to immortalize his queen, Mumtaj Mahal, by creating the glorious Taj Mahal. Although the Taj Mahal has withstood the ravages of time for three centuries, and might continue to stand for a long time to come, ultimately it will come down one day.

Death does not wait for anyone. We find that daily, kings and queens, politicians and religious heads, all have to succumb to it; nobody can escape death. Life appears to be a game of musical chairs wherein at every round another chair is taken away and someone loses his seat. Similarly, each time I meet my friends and relations I find that another chair has been vacated and another acquaintance or relation has died.

Death is not only inevitable, it is also a painful

process. The Hindu scriptures say that the pain a person
has to undergo at the time of death equals the
simultaneous stinging of a million scorpions. Again, the
holy Koran likens the anguish through which we have to
pass at the time of death to that experienced by inserting
a thorny shrub into the rectum and taking it out through
the mouth. The twelfth century saint Baba Farid has
said that at the time of death every one of our limbs
aches, twists and breaks.

St. Paul has said that death is the last enemy we have
to conquer. So let us consider how we can avoid the
pain and anguish of death, and how we can attain true
immortality which is an intrinsic desire of every human
being.

The Sikh scriptures say that when we are born, God
Almighty gives us a *poonji*, or capital, which is the
amount of time allotted to us in our earthly sojourn. We
should make the best use of that capital by finding a
way to conquer death and solving life's mystery, but
instead we remain in deep slumber like Rip Van Winkle.
Kabir Sahib explains that we remain in this slumber of
mind, matter and illusion until the Angel of Death
strikes us on our head with a rod and wakes us up. But
by that time it is too late. It is a pity that while living in
the world we forget the reality of death. The Gurbani
has said, "Life is falsehood and death is the only
reality." We have forgotten that we are souls, and not
the body. We consider ourselves to be the body and we
become engrossed in the sensuous pleasures of mind
and matter. We do not realize that the body is a rented
house which we occupy only for a limited period before
it must be vacated. Hazur Baba Sawan Singh and Sant

Kirpal Singh used to say that we are blessed with this human body after being separated from God for trillions of years. It is a special privilege that He has given us this human life, which is known in the scriptures to be the crown of creation. It is the highest in all creation because it is only in this form that the soul can rise above body-consciousness, traverse through the inner planes and attain self-knowledge and God-realization. But how many of us make the best use of the time allotted to us in life? Most of us awaken when it is too late; a golden opportunity has been lost. If we want immortal life, if we want eternal peace, bliss and ecstasy, if we want to attain eternal salvation, then we have to solve the mystery of life and death while we are living in this body.

The question remains: How can we solve these mysteries? All religions give us a clue—they refer to the Word or Naam. When God came into expression He assumed two forms. One was the Light of God, and the other was the Music of the Spheres. This Celestial Music has been called the *Word* in the Bible: "In the beginning was the Word, and the Word was with God, and the Word was God." The Hindu Vedas call it *Naad, Jyoti* and *Sruti*. The Muslim Sufis call it *Kalam-i-Qadim*, or *Kalma*. The Zoroastrians call it *Sraosha*. The Buddhists call it *Sonorous Light*. The Sikhs call it *Naam, Shabd, Kirtan, Bani* and *Jyot*. All these religions refer to the Word or Naam as the Power of God, emanating from the Absolute, which is the cause and sustainer of all creation. It is the Power of God that keeps the universes going, and controls us in the body. Just as this Power flows outward from God, that same Current flows back to its source. This Power, in the form of Light and Sound, can be contacted at the seat of the soul between and behind the two eyes. It acts like a magnet and draws the spirit to itself. If the soul were not covered by the rust of mind and matter it would go up in an instant. The Current would then take the soul along its course through the higher regions, passing through the astral and causal planes, until it reached its source in the pure spiritual regions. The question now is: How to get access to this Current? For this we have to go to an adept, a living Master, who has himself solved the mystery of life and death and can help us solve it in this very lifetime.

He teaches us the process of meditation. Through his own attention he can help us withdraw our attention from the nine apertures or outer doors of the physical body, so that it comes up to the center of the soul at the tenth door, known as the single eye or third eye. He pulls asunder the veil, and our inner eye is opened to see the Light of God, and our inner ear is opened to hear the Celestial Harmony of all Harmonies reverberating within. This firsthand spiritual experience is given by a living Master on the day of initiation into the mysteries of the Beyond. If we are fortunate enough to come to such a Master, we will not only succeed in rising above body-consciousness, thereby conquering death, but will also succeed in attaining our ultimate communion with God.

The process of inversion of the senses during meditation is the same process that we undergo at the time of death when the sensory currents withdraw from the body. In both processes the currents first start withdrawing from the toes, feet, and legs, and come upwards, and we find that our feet and legs grow numb. Then the navel, heart and throat centers of the body progressively become numb. Then the soul enters the eye-center. Finally, it passes out of the body from the eye-center. So the most significant point for concentrating in meditation is at the eye-focus, which is the last place our soul comes to before leaving the body.

Concentration at this point between and behind the two eyes is the basis of the meditation practiced by the saints of Surat Shabd Yoga or Sant Mat—the Path of the Masters. By concentrating at this point, we attain bliss; we traverse the higher inner regions until we reach a stage where the soul at last sees that it is of the same essence as God, and attains self-knowledge. The soul is then ready to move to its ultimate goal—merger with the Absolute, or God-realization. There we attain all bliss, all peace, all ecstasy, and achieve true immortality. This is the stage which the prophets and saints of the world have called the be-all and end-all of human life.

St. Plutarch has said that the souls of those initiated into the mysteries of the Beyond have the same experience of leaving the body as at the time of death. So the process of withdrawal of the soul from the body, which we undergo at the time of our physical death, is the same process we can practice during our lifetime, when we learn to meditate under the guidance of a living Master. That is why it is called "dying while living." It has been said, "Learn to die so that you may begin to live." This art of learning to die while living has been stated to be the panacea for all ills which the human body passes through at the time of death. The great saints and seers have all stressed the need to learn the art of dying while living. The Muslim scriptures say, "Die before death." Socrates said true philosophers are "always occupied in the practice of dying." The Indian saint, Dadu Sahib, has said, "O Dadu, we all must die eventually, but why not learn to master death while living?" The saints practice this "dying while living" many times a day at will. They can rise above body-consciousness, soar into the higher regions and return to the body in a twinkling of an eye.

This process has been aptly described by the Muslims as *intaqal*, meaning "a change from one place to another." In the customs of the Hindus and Sikhs, death is called the *chola badalna* or "changing of the garment." Death is only a transition. In some scriptures death is described as a period of rest between journeys. Some call it the period of judgment between one life and another.

In their writings, the saints and mystics have described what happens after death to those who have not come to a perfect Master. According to their deeds they go to paradise, hell, or *ahraf*—an area intervening between heaven and hell. When the prescribed period of their stay is over, they return to the cycle of rebirths. If they are lucky enough to receive initiation from a perfect living Master, then all the records of their deeds are transferred from the Angel of Death to the living Master, and the Master becomes the arbiter of their destiny. In that case, those souls will not be reborn below the human level. After death they will either stay on the higher planes and complete their inner journey back to God from there, or the Master may prescribe for them another human birth in which their meditations can be perfected.

The human body is the golden opportunity given to us in which to know God and attain immortality. Those who do not have communion with God as the aim of their lives, those who do not consider attaining ultimate salvation as the summum bonum of their lives, those who do not consider it a dire necessity to attain immortality in their lives, and who fall an easy prey to mind and matter, passing their lives engrossed in the sensuous pleasures, are prone to return to lower forms of life. They are prone to fall from the highest point of the cycle of births and deaths.

Unfortunately, we waste this golden opportunity. Our scriptures tell us that God made man in His own image, and that man is superior to the angels. It is said that when man was created, God asked the angels to pay obeisance to the human form. If the angels want salvation, even they must be born as human beings, because it is only in the human form that one can realize God.

We can attain our ultimate victory over death by coming to the feet of a living Master. Once we go to a perfect Master, then all the pains and afflictions that man generally faces at the time of death are taken care of, and we leave the physical body blissfully and peacefully. Instead of the Angel of Death, our Master himself appears in his inner radiant form and takes our soul to the higher planes.

The great saint Kabir Sahib has said, "The death which other people are afraid of is a source of per-

manent bliss for me. It is only by passing this stage that
I attain eternal peace, eternal bliss and eternal
salvation."

As Socrates prepared for death, his friends wept,
but he declared, "When I have come to the end of my
journey, I shall attain that which has been the pursuit of
my life. And therefore I go on my way rejoicing."

Among the Sufis the death anniversary of a saint is
known as an *urs*, or marriage. At death the mystics do
not say that a saint has died, they say that he has attained union with God.

One poet, Shamim Karhani, has said:

> *The festivity of birth is over, and the*
> *festivity of death is yet to come;*
> *One marriage party has already come, and*
> *the other marriage party is yet to arrive.*

We have had the festivities of being born into this
world, and at the time of initiation by our spiritual
Master we are born anew and reenter the Kingdom of
God. Now we are waiting for the final festivity which
will accompany our death, because it is only by passing
through this change that we attain final communion
with God. In the case of saints, and their disciples who
have learned to merge with God, the time of death is
really the time of their spiritual marriage. So if we are
able to solve this mystery of life and death during our
lifetime, and "learn to die so that we may begin to
live," then the time of death becomes the time of joy.

It is therefore imperative that we carefully consider
the mystery of life and death, and the journey we all
must take. This is the most important, yet the most

ignored aspect of a person's life. In our daily lives, when we go on even a small journey, we look through guidebooks to see what the climate will be like and what clothes we should take with us. We read about the places that we will be visiting. If when we take a small journey, we prepare for it; why then do we remain ignorant about the greatest journey in our lives?

Saints and seers have been stressing that we should be prepared for the journey from this life to another. On that journey we cannot take anything with us. All our worldly possessions, all our worldly belongings, all our relatives and friends are left behind. Nothing can come with us. We go alone, and the only baggage that we can take with us is the package of human qualities and godly qualities which we have developed in our lives.

We should awaken to the truth that our time is also coming. Who knows when we are going to end this journey and start another one? Who knows, the world may end tonight. Who knows whether we are going to take the next breath or not? Once during my government service a fellow officer was discussing a case with me for half an hour. A few moments after I left him and returned to my office, his secretary called to say that my colleague was in critical condition. By the time I reached his office, he had died. Suddenly and unexpectedly he had finished his journey and started another.

Have we not wasted enough of the precious capital which was granted to us? Whatever time is left to us, let us make the most of it. If we learn to rise above body-consciousness we can prepare ourselves for this final change from one life to another. We have seen that death is inevitable; nobody can ever escape it. Saints and seers, kings and queens, those gifted in the finer arts in life, those who are involved in any pursuit, one and all, have to pass through the same gate—the gate of death. We can begin now to ready ourselves for this journey by preparing our baggage of human and godly qualities. We are micro-gods. In a rudimentary form, in a dormant state, we have within us all the heavenly attributes. All that we have to do is ignite the fire within, and that igniting of the inner torch can only be done by an adept in the science of the soul. Let us resolve, and not only resolve but act on this resolution, that when the final change comes, we will have already solved the inner mysteries, and achieved the conquest of death.

CHAPTER THREE
SHORTCUTS
TO
SPIRITUALITY

If we are interested in traversing the spiritual path, we are faced with an important question. There are so many yogas, so many practices, so many ways of finding God; which way should we follow? A comparative study of religion and yoga shows that all paths agree in affirming that we have to learn to die while living in order to attain eternal life. Scores of books have been written recently by scientists, doctors and psychologists showing that it *is* possible to have a transcendent experience. But the question is, how can we do it at will? And once we have this spiritual experience, how can we continue the inner journey in our lifetime until we reach the stages of self-knowledge and God-realization?

All religions, yogas and spiritual paths have taught how this journey back to God can be undertaken. But each path has its own merits, and we should consider these if we want to complete this inner journey within our short life span.

Ours is an age of shortcuts. In every home, wherever

we go, we see books expounding shortcuts to understanding various topics, such as shortcuts to success,
to perfection, to the attainment of a working knowledge
of economics. In the past we did not have these shortcuts, and we had to do things the long way. For
example, for each subject at school we had to read all
the standard books, which involved a lot of time and
labor. We had to master eight to twelve books on each
subject. But in this modern age, studying is much easier
because of books such as *Shortcuts to Success in
Chemistry*, and *Shortcuts to Success in History*.

We also have shortcuts in transportation. In the old
days it took two months to travel by ship from India to
America. If by some chance there was a storm, the
turbulent waves could force the ship to cast anchor at
some place along the way, causing further delay. And
one can imagine the time it took if the ship drifted off
course. But now we can travel that same distance by jet
in a matter of hours.

The basic principles of spirituality are eternal and do
not change with the passage of time, but in this modern
age we do need shortcuts to reach the goal of self-
knowledge and realization of God. In the past these
shortcuts were not necessary—the scriptures describe
how the rishis, munis and seers of old were blessed with
long lives of sixty-five thousand or eighty thousand
years. So they could devote thousands of years to
meditation. In those days they were following the path
which involved breath control. But the path which took
breath control into consideration was a very long one. It
took thousands of years to attain certain stages of
spirituality, and even then the yogis, munis and rishis

did not reach perfection. Often, the first time they were tested they slipped and fell.

The basic principles of spirituality remain the same, but according to the *zeitgeist*, or the spirit of the age, techniques change. For example, some of the yogas require extreme asceticism, but this cannot be followed by most people in the modern world. Especially for the elderly, the infirm and for children, many yogic practices are difficult and include techniques which require a strong body. One must sit straight with the backbone stretched, or adopt certain postures or asanas. Will the elderly or people in poor physical health be able to practice such yogas? Even if we are able to perform these now, what will happen in a few decades if poor health or the infirmities of old age overtake us? We would not be able to perform these practices any longer.

God is not so limited, not so unjust, that He requires a path that bans the very young and the very old. Spirituality is not the sole privilege of youth with strong, healthy bodies. The true path to God can be practiced by all, is available to all, from the very young to the elderly. We need to bear this in mind when searching for a path back to God.

There are a multitude of yogas and each one is trying to reach the same goal. It is not that God can be reached by only one path; God can be reached by many, and each path has its own merits. All paths lead to God, but the point is that in the short span of life given to us we have to cover the entire spiritual journey in order to reach God. In this age of shortcuts, we need the shortest, most reliable path in spirituality also.

Taking into account our vulnerability, our weaknesses, and our short life span in this modern age, the pioneers of Sant Mat have taught a method which bypasses the trials and tribulations of more familiar yogas. The yogic exercises which were prevalent entailed an intensive, long period of meditation before anyone could achieve the ultimate goal. But during a period which coincided with the Renaissance in Europe, two great Masters, Guru Nanak and Kabir Sahib, appeared in India and taught a shortcut to spirituality: Surat Shabd Yoga. This is the yoga taught by the adepts of Sant Mat, the Path of the Masters.

The basic theory of Sant Mat is that our body consists of two currents: the motor and the sensory. The motor current deals with the growth of our hair and nails, our breathing, our digestion, and the circulation of our blood. Various yogas try to control the motor current through breathing exercises and physical postures. But the pioneers of Sant Mat dispensed with the methods of breath control. When we are busy attending to any task in life, we are not aware of our breathing. Are we aware of our breathing when we work in our offices, when we produce music, poetry or art, or when we talk to our friends? Supposing we meet our beloved and have a love-prate, are we conscious of our breathing then? When we talk to our beloved we begin to lose ourselves, and become oblivious to our breathing, our self and our surroundings. At the outset we may be aware of the fragrant flowers, the blossoming buds, and the starry skies all around; but when the love-prate begins, within minutes we become totally oblivious of our environment. If in our ordinary functions in life we do not attend to the motor current and the breathing, why should we pay attention to it while we are meditating, while we are supposed to be engaged in a love-prate with our Eternal Beloved? Whatever is true of worldly lovers, at least that much must be true of our behavior when we start meditating on God and communing with Him. This is why the Masters of Sant Mat do not take breath control into consideration in their meditation practices. They do not say that the path of breath control is wrong, only that it is an unnecessarily long and arduous one.

The Masters who teach Surat Shabd Yoga concern themselves only with the sensory current. This is the current which provides us with the sensation of feeling. When the sensory currents are spread out in the limbs, we have the sensation of feeling. But when they withdraw from the extremities, the limbs become numb. The purpose of meditation is to withdraw the sensory currents from the body to the seat of the soul, so we can rise above body-consciousness, enter the Beyond, traverse the higher planes, and attain self-knowledge and God-realization. This process of rising above body-consciousness is known by the mystics as "dying while living." It is the same process undergone at the time of physical death when the sensory currents withdraw, except that during meditation the silver cord connecting our soul to the body does not break, and we return to the body at will. If we want to attain our spiritual goal, we must learn to rise above body-consciousness, and this is achieved by the process of inverting our attention during meditation.

If we compare the different yogic systems we find

that some begin their concentration, their meditation, at the lower chakras in the body. There are six chakras, the lowest being at the juncture between the legs and the trunk, which is the center of the kundalini. Those who practice kundalini yoga begin their concentration at that point. Their sensory currents begin to withdraw from the toes and legs, and those portions become numb as at the time of death. But during meditation and at the time of death, the process of withdrawal does not stop with the kundalini center. When the sensory currents come above the kundalini center, the kundalini stops functioning and itself becomes numb, but the man is still alive. During the further withdrawal from the body, the currents next come to the navel center. Other yogas begin their concentration here; they generate a deep sound from the navel. Yet when someone withdraws above the navel, that center also becomes numb and stops functioning even though the man is still alive. By this time the death of the kundalini is past history. Then the sensory currents withdraw to the heart center, the gullet and the tongue; each one in turn becomes numb and ceases to function, yet the man is still alive. Many practices begin their point of concentration at the tongue, where the repetition of holy mantras goes on. But when the withdrawal of the currents continues, this center also stops functioning. Next, the currents withdraw above the nose and come to the eyes. Finally, the sensory currents reach the last point before transcending the physical body. This center or chakra is between and behind the two eyebrows, and is called the center of the soul. It is also referred to as the still point, the third eye or single eye, the *tisra til, shiv netra, divya chakshu* or the tenth door. When the currents reach this point the pupils first turn upwards, and then downwards, and we say at that time the soul has finally left the body.

Now, we can see for ourselves that the kundalini center, and the other lower centers, stop functioning long before the man has left the body. It is not the lower center, but the point between the two eyes which is the last center our soul passes through before leaving the body.

If we start meditating at the kundalini chakra and then slowly go from one chakra to the other, before rising up to the point where we finally transcend the body, it is a long process. It requires a great amount of time and effort to rise from the lower centers to the center of the soul. In this short span of life of about fifty to seventy years, we can hardly expect to reach our goal. So the saints of modern times, instead of starting at the very base, and then working their way up, start with the highest point—the third eye or single eye. The basic requirements remain the same, but by changing the center from the kundalini to the eye-focus, the saints have clearly given us the shortest possible way. They tell us we should make the jump to the center of the soul.

Every year we find in the sphere of athletics that old records are broken—pole-vaulters and jumpers are reaching higher and higher heights. In my time the high-jump record was far lower than it is now. The hundred-yard run took a much longer time than it does now. So in these times we should master the new techniques which have enabled athletes to surpass previous records. In spirituality, too, we should make the jump from a lower center to the highest center, the point between and behind the two eyebrows. It is at this center that the real heart of the mystics exists. If we read Hafiz, Attar, Shamas-e-Tabrez or Maulana Rumi, we will find that according to them the real heart of the mystic is the center of the soul. It is not the lump of flesh the size of one's fist. It has a much vaster expanse because this is the fountainhead of love in the physical body. The saints always teach a method of meditation which involves concentration of the attention at this center.

According to the Surat Shabd Yoga, or the science of the soul, the basis of meditation is the attention. "Surat" means "attention." "Shabd," known as the Word or Logos, is the "Sound Current." And "Yoga" means "union with God." Masters show us the process of uniting our attention, which is the outward expression of the soul, with God through the Sound Current. When the attention is withdrawn from the five senses, the senses do not work. We know that when we are deep in thought, our eyes may be open, but they do not see who is passing by. When we are absorbed in thought, our ears are open but we may not hear someone calling us. Similarly, in meditation, by concentrating our attention on the center of the soul, the senses cease to function—we become dead to the world, but alive within.

No difficult posture is necessary for this practice. We are to sit in any pose which is most convenient, in which there is no tension in any part of the body. Then we are to look intently and lovingly into the darkness lying in front of us, without putting any strain on our eyes or forehead. We should then be perfectly relaxed, but at the same time, we should be wide-awake, with the attention focused intently at the seat of the soul behind the two eyes. At the time of initiation, the Master gives the disciple five Charged Names which are to be repeated slowly and at short intervals with the tongue of thought so as not to disturb the inner gaze.

The repetition of these five holy Names is called *simran*. Simran is repetition of the Names of God which have been charged with the thought transference or attention of a living Master. The Names have the power to still the mind, and help us rise above body-consciousness. In some spiritual practices people engage in simran with the aid of a rosary, but in that type of simran the attention remains divided. One has to roll the beads with the fingers, and eventually the fingers are able to do this automatically, while the unbridled mind continues to wander astray. Many people do simran with their tongue, but the tongue ends up moving in the mouth while the mind continues to run riot. Some do simran at the thyroid gland, but this is also not effective when the attention does not remain fully rivetted to it. Others do simran at the heart center, but the mind still has a chance to run amuck. This is why Masters of Surat Shabd Yoga prescribe the simran done by tongue of thought—mental simran—which is the easiest way to withdraw the soul from the body. Maulana Rumi, the great Sufi saint, said *zikr*, or simran of the highest type, is that which helps in manifesting the reality within—*zikr-e-ruhe*, simran done with full attention. Rishi Shandilya in his Upanishad says that *manasiki* (simran) done mentally with the tongue of thought is the best of all simrans.

The Charged Names given by the Master are repeated slowly and mentally. This practice inverts the mind and weans it away from worldly thoughts and mundane matters until it achieves a state of equipoise. This stilling of the mind brings the sensory currents up to the eye-center. The other current in the body, the motor current, which is responsible for breathing, the functioning of the digestive system, growth, and blood circulation, is not affected. These bodily functions continue to go on automatically while we are in meditation. It is only the sensory currents which are systematically withdrawn and gathered up at one point—the eye-focus—for penetration and transcendence into the Beyond.

When we have withdrawn to the eye-focus we begin to see the Light of God. The inner experience of Light in the early stages may not be so radiant, but as one progresses and goes higher, the Light becomes more and more effulgent. We then become more absorbed in the Light, and begin to cross the inner moon, sun, and stars until we reach the radiant form of our Master within. When the radiant or astral form of the Master appears, it is the greatest blessing because it will certainly still the mind, which by nature does not want to be stilled. As we proceed further, we become disentangled from the pull of the mind and senses, and we find that the radiant form becomes more and more resplendent. It becomes so absorbing that we merge in that form, a stage known in Sufism as *fana-fil-sheikh*, or merger in the Master. We now begin to enter realms which are beyond the power of words to describe. We derive great ecstasy, bliss and peace as we transcend the higher spiritual regions, crossing the astral, causal and supracausal planes until we reach our ultimate goal, which is the second stage in mysticism called *fana-fil-Allah*, or merger in God.

The second meditation practice given by the Masters of Surat Shabd Yoga is contact with the inner Sound. While keeping the attention at the eye-focus one can listen to the Sound Current which at first appears to be coming from the right side. The Sound eventually becomes louder and louder and begins to pull the spirit up. This magical Sound which is reverberating ceaselessly within us can be heard when a competent Master frees us from the entanglement of mind and senses and lifts our soul above body-consciousness. At each inner stage the Celestial Music becomes more and more enrapturing. When the soul hears this divine strain it gets magnetized and attracted to it with the result that the mind and senses are stilled, and the spirit rises up. There are five different melodies, each relating to a distinct spiritual region, and they lead us from one spiritual plane to another until the true home of the soul, known as Sach Khand, is reached. By becoming absorbed in these five melodies, one is led from stage to stage. Once the soul reaches the final stage, salvation is assured and the cycle of births and deaths ends.

This is the grand purpose of life which one can attain in this very lifetime through the help of a living Master. By day-to-day practice one can increase his inner experiences of the Light and Sound of God until one can transcend and return to body-consciousness at will. The more time devoted to the spiritual practices, the easier it becomes to withdraw from the body at will.

The Masters of Surat Shabd Yoga do not require us to leave the world and to seek a cave; they do not impose austerities and practices which only the few can honor. The path they offer is at once the simplest, the shortest and the most natural for attaining our spiritual goal.

CHAPTER FOUR
PERFECT SCIENTIST

To conquer death, we have to learn how to rise above body-consciousness at will. The method for doing this is a science: the science of spirituality. It is, in fact, a perfect science which each of us can verify for ourself. The only laboratory we need is that of the human body. The question before us is: How can we learn to master this science?

If we want to learn physics, a physics teacher who lived in the past cannot help us understand the subject. But if we go to a living professor of physics, we will find combined in him all that was taught by past professors, and all the latest concepts now taught in different countries. Further, if we want to perform an experiment in atomic physics we cannot do so by the mere reading of books. We have to go to a professor; and we will want to seek out the greatest living exponent of atomic physics in our times. In the same way, if we want to perform the experiment of dying while living, we need to go to the most competent living teacher, call him by any name: Saint, Guide, Murshid, Guru, Master.

Just consider, if we wished to learn the theory of relativity and we lived in Einstein's time, would we have gone to anybody else? Now that Einstein is no longer with us, if we wish to master the theory of relativity we will have difficulty understanding it on our own by only reading about it. The theory of relativity is not so simple. We will need the help of some living professor of that subject. And even then, it is not just a question of understanding theory; it is a question of performing experiments, and experiencing the science for ourselves. We honor the old writings of past professors, old scriptures, prophets, saints and seers; but if we want the experience for ourselves, we need the help of a living teacher in the science.

By saying we need a living Master we do not denigrate past Masters, because they were also once the living Masters of their times. But religion is no longer a question of blind belief, rites, rituals, or of going by the statements given in the old scriptures. The days of blind belief are gone.

It is the greatest gift of the two great Masters, Baba Sawan Singh and Sant Kirpal Singh, that they presented spirituality to the modern world as a perfect science. Just as we perform a scientific experiment in a laboratory, so too, we can perform the experiment of rising above body-consciousness to gain self-knowledge and God-realization, in the laboratory which God has made, the laboratory of the human body. God does not reside in temples made by human hands; He resides in the temple He has fashioned Himself—the human body.

The outer temples and churches were made from the

model of the human body. They are usually dome-shaped and forehead-shaped; sometimes, as in churches, they are cross-shaped, or shaped like the long bridge of the nose. In the temples and churches there are two symbols: one of light and the other of sound. Candles and eternal flames represent the Light of God within man, and bells, drums, and conches symbolize the Celestial Sound within. These outer lights and sounds are only to remind man that the Light of God and the Music of the Spheres can be found within the true temple which is the human body. But we have become lost in the rites, rituals and symbols, and have forgotten their original meaning.

Both man and God reside in this divine temple, but unfortunately they are like a husband and wife who share the same bed but cannot see each other. So if we wish to perform the experiment of self-knowledge and God-realization, we must learn to enter this laboratory and contact the Light and Sound within.

To perform this experiment we want the most competent Master, irrespective of his religion or nationality. If we are working on an important science project we will go to the most competent scientist irrespective of the country from which he comes. We will go to him regardless of his religion. If we want to learn this science of the soul completely, we will try to find out who the best teacher is, whether he is a Zoroastrian, Buddhist, Sikh, Christian, Hindu, Moslem or Jew. We have to rise above such dualities. As spirituality is a science, we will go to the most competent exponent not only for theoretical explanations, but also for the practical experience.

When we go to a competent scientist or professor, there is no question of conversion in order to study under him. A scientist does not give us any particular religion. He will tell us to remain Christian, if we are Christian; he will tell us to remain Jewish, if we are Jewish; he will tell us to remain Moslem, if we are Moslem. We will continue being Sikh, if we are Sikh, and the same applies to any other religion to which we may belong. The concept that a Master belongs to a set pattern, a set religion, a set nationality, or a set creed is not correct. What he gives us is a principle—the principle of initiation. And then he gives a practical experience of the principle.

So just as a competent professor of physics will teach all students, no matter what their race or nationality, and will not ask them to convert, a perfect living Master will not espouse the necessity of conversion in order to study the spiritual science. If anyone believes in conversion he is not a true Master. Whatever our religion, we can receive the guidance of a Master and have a practical experience of self-knowledge and God-realization.

Spirituality is simple: It is comprised of theory and practical experience by which we can verify the theory for ourselves. Originally the prophets and saints, those we call the founders of the various religions, knew the inner truth and could give a practical experience of it to their followers. But in due course, these prophets and saints left the earth, and their followers did not seek out their successors—the living teachers. As a result, those who became the religious leaders—the ministers, mullahs, and pundits— eventually lost that touch, that personal inner experience, and were left only with theory. And when left only with the theory, the religious leaders were always afraid that someone would come along and ask them for a practical inner spiritual experience. As a result they began creating rites and rituals to make spirituality seem more and more complicated. People became so lost in this labyrinth of rites and rituals that they were never able to come out of it, never able to ask searching questions, never able to experience communion of soul with God. And this has been the fate of all religions. The exoteric side of religions, consisting of rites and rituals, grows at a very rapid speed, while the esoteric side, which is the real core consisting of inner mystical experiences, vanishes and goes into oblivion. So in order to conceal their own ignorance, and because they could not give any practical experience, ministers, pundits, and mullahs went on adding ritual after ritual. Eventually they lost their clarity of expression and took recourse to verbosity and the use of high-sounding words clarifying nothing.

If we really want a firsthand experience of spirituality, we will find out who the most competent teacher is. In the realm of education, if we want to study under the best teacher in a given field, we will go to him no matter which institution he teaches in. Similarly, in the science of spirituality, we are not interested in which institution of religion, or to which country the most renowned teacher belongs. If we are sincere, we will go to him. Spirituality is a pure science. It is a pure principle of experiencing communion with God, of receiving a firsthand inner experience of the Light of God and the Music of the Spheres on the day of initiation.

A perfect living Master is able to give a disciple a contact with the divine Light and the Harmony of all Harmonies because he has become one with God and works as a conscious co-worker of the divine plan. A perfect Master, under instructions and guidance from his own teacher, is able to separate his soul from his body, traverse the inner regions, and reach the source of all Light, thereby merging with God. He can return to his body in the twinkling of an eye. To help man reach the same goal of God-realization, God has been sending perfect saints and Masters since time immemorial.

Because God, the Universal Power which permeates creation as Word or Naam, is invisible to man, He cannot give man guidance except by working through a human pole. Man cannot learn from an unseen Creator unless he rises to His level. Man alone can be the teacher of man. Therefore, God in His compassion gives a direct commission to certain souls to work in the material world in order to perform the sacred duty of bringing seekers after truth back to Him. Such commissioned souls have been called saints or Masters.

God Power, Christ Power, or Master Power has existed in all times and is the same, but it has been working at different human poles. This world has never been without a living Master or a living Christ since creation came into being. At one time the Christ Power worked at the pole of Buddha, and at another time, at the pole of Mahavira; it has worked at the pole of Jesus, and at other times it has worked at the pole of Mohammed, Zoroaster, Kabir, Guru Nanak, Guru Arjan Dev, Guru Gobind Singh, Baba Sawan Singh and

Sant Kirpal Singh. The Christ Power continues working now, and will continue working in the future; only the poles will change.

Although physically the past saints are no longer with us, the God Power or Christ Power which spoke through them lives on. Unfortunately, many people believe that the particular prophet or saint they revere was the last one. The Muslims say that Mohammed was the last, yet they admit that there were many prophets before Mohammed. If prophets could grace the earth before him, why shouldn't there be any after him? A similar case is made by the Christians; but if there were so many prophets before Jesus, what is there that would debar God from sending any more prophets after him? Every formal religion claims its prophet or Christ to be the last. This has created dissensions, crusades, religious wars, atrocities, strife and fanaticism resulting in bloodshed all over the world. As a result of this fanatic attitude, in order to raise one mosque, or one church, or one temple of bricks, we have razed to the ground millions of true churches, millions of true mosques, millions of human beings—the real temples of God. Is God so unjust that He will commission only *one* Prophet or Christ for *one* people in *one* given time in eternity, and not send another savior for the people who came to the earth before him or after him? If we say, "Yes, that is so," then we have cut at the root of the belief in all prophets who came before the one in whom we believe. Even the Bible says that we respect *all* the prophets God has sent. If there was only a need for one prophet, what was the necessity of God sending so many? God should have sent him in the very beginning, and that would have been the end of it. But if God has provided previous generations with saviors, why shouldn't our present generation be blessed with one, and why should posterity be devoid of that blessing?

There is no end to the coming of the saints. Nature's inexorable and eternal law of demand and supply always works. There is food for the hungry and water for the thirsty.

CHAPTER FIVE

BOAT
OF
NAAM

We are suffering unprecedented floods in Delhi and in many other parts of the country. Within minutes, countless homes have been darkened, and news has come in giving appalling stories of people who have been drowned. The government issued warnings at various places and asked the people to take adequate measures, as it was known that a great flood was coming. The authorities said very clearly that the quickly rising waters could become a danger to life and property, and if the people did not take heed at once they would become the victims of the fury of the flood.

Now we find that those who heeded these warnings and moved to safe ground were secure; their houses may have been damaged or even totally washed away, but they themselves were saved. Those who did not heed the warnings were drowned or found themselves in great difficulties, having lost their property and in the grip of fever or disease. This flood has caused much havoc, many misfortunes, and great damage and destruction.

In the same way, we too have to search for some safe

ground for ourselves—a place which is undisturbed by the turbulent twists of Nature. It must be a place free from the turmoil of this world. It must be a place free from the material problems of this physical existence; it must be free from the vulnerability of the human body. We have to find such a place which offers peace to everyone, harmony to everyone, welfare to everyone. The happiness we shall enjoy there is, of course, unlike any fleeting happiness we may encounter in this sad world. The happiness of that place is totally unaffected by any change of climate or the fury of Nature. It is a happiness which is eternal and knows no change.

Just as the government warned us of the impending flood and its danger, so a Higher Government warns us of the impending tragedy of our worldly life. Divine teachers are sent to arouse mankind and alert us to the dangers. They come to tell us that we have attained human birth, which is itself a rare privilege, and having been granted the boon of human existence we have reached the high point on the Wheel of Life—the round of transmigration. They exhort us to seek refuge in the protective fold of a divine Boatman who can safely ferry us across the turmoil and catastrophies of this earth life. There is no time to be lost; every moment, every second is precious. These divine saviors come to serve us; they charge no fees; they ask nothing of us but to heed their warnings and sail with them to eternal safety. But we hardly listen to their pleas, although we know in our heart of hearts that this is the only way to attain permanent peace, permanent contentment, permanent salvation.

What is the ultimate outcome of this folly? We have

been helplessly watching the distress of the people who did not heed the government's warnings about the coming flood. Just as those who disregarded those urgent warnings have been swept away and their bodies now float on the raging waters, so are our lives caught in a mad whirl of earthly activities, being wasted and destroyed on the high floods of *maya*, illusion. Our lives are rushing towards their end without bearing fruit as we lose the opportunity for salvation offered us by the divine Boatman who is searching for us—pleading with us—to enter his unsinkable boat: the boat of Naam, the eternal Word of God.

Some of you have seen the flooded areas. Some of you have visited the affected places. You have seen how the government sent out special boats, and how those who availed themselves of such boats have been brought to safety. Some of those boats are still plying the waters looking for survivors; they are all government boats. Have you come across any marooned family that managed to escape by using its own boat? Who keeps a boat in the middle of a city? Only those who entrusted themselves to the assistance offered by the government were able to save their lives and some of their precious belongings.

So we, too, have to reach beyond the limits of the flood of time; we have to find a place where the Lord of Death has no power and where his agents cannot trap us. But who can reach this haven of safety? only those rare ones who have found a master Boatman able to row them across the treacherous waters. Any individual who thinks he can make this journey on his own is sadly mistaken. We all need the assistance of an expert

Boatman, the divine Boatman who knows all about the eddies, the whirlpools and other hazards. We need the assistance of the savior who has been sent by the Higher Government and is aware of the treachery of the furious waters. Only such a one can ensure that we reach our cherished goal.

Nature is seeking to teach us by every means at its command. Every little leaf in this world seeks to put across a moral to us. But because of our indifference, because of our abandonment to attachment and illusion, we find that even these drastic flood waters cannot awaken us to the vulnerable plight we are in. We strive so hard to possess all sorts of objects to make our lives pleasanter, easier; but they break, we tire of them, or we lose them. What we treasured yesterday, today has little meaning or causes much pain. We struggle from one disappointment to another, but we still procrastinate. When it is time for meditation, we put it off for the next day. We think that everything will wait for us. When we are students, we tell ourselves we will engage in the spiritual practices after we have completed our exams. When we have passed the exams, we say we will take up the instructions of the Guru in all seriousness after we have found a job. When a job has been found, then we want to wait until after marriage. The whole spiritual pursuit goes on being endlessly postponed.

In the sacred city of Benares, the great saint Kabir Sahib used to visit a man who liked to pass his day sitting in his garden. Kabir urged him to spend his time improving himself by engaging in his spiritual practices. At first this man replied, "My children are still young; I will turn to the devotion of God when they are grown up." Years later, Kabir asked the man, "Dear friend, you surely must be enjoying your practices now?" The man replied, "You see, I am waiting for all my children to be married; then I will devote myself entirely to meditation." Later, when Kabir went to visit the man again, he asked, "Now that all your children are married, how fortunate you are. Are you really spending all your time in meditation?" The reply was, "Not yet, because I am so keen to see my grandchildren grow up and get settled." Some years later when Kabir again went to see his friend, he was told that the man had died. Kabir, turning to the grandchildren, said, "That poor man wasted his whole life in this garden listening to the orders of his worldly mind."

As followers of this material world we always find some excuse or other to put off doing our spiritual practices. But who knows if, like the victims of the flood, the world will end for us this very night? The life that has been given us is fickle indeed; who can say when it will give us the slip! I am now addressing you, but can I be certain that I will be able to speak the next words I have in mind? People have been known to die in the middle of a sentence. It is for this reason that the saints have always stressed that we must give up our habit of putting off things until tomorrow. Sant Kirpal Singh used to say, "Procrastination is the thief of time." But we do not care to listen to the divine teachers. They tell us repeatedly that what we mean to do tomorrow should be done today, and what we plan to do today should be done here and now. But instead of listening to them, we go on carelessly wasting the precious life that has been given to us. Instead of devoting ourselves to the worship of the Father so as to become reunited with Him, we lose ourselves in the false security of the world, and we worship material things.

Nature seeks to teach us at every turn. If only the vibrations from her dancing fingers could touch the strings of our heart, we would throb to her divine Music and it would awaken us from our long slumber. If anyone, indeed, can touch the strings of our heart, it is a realized one, a perfect Master. He knows the inmost depths of the heart, the inmost depths of the soul. He knows the subtlest of the subtle, and he alone can help us to become attuned to the Music of the Universe. This magical Sound cannot be heard by everyone. Ordinary mortals are deaf to that inner Music, for it is only the divine teacher who can give us the sensitivity to respond to its mysterious call. One of my verses is:

*All glory to the Beloved who has
    broken my heart!
For the music of its breaking has
    shattered the silence of the night.*

Even the breaking of a heart has its own sound, and for those who have the ear, it is audible.

We have to learn to hear the resounding Music—the Music of the Creator. We have to learn to hear its unending melody. In that way we can awaken from the sleep we have fallen into—the slumber of illusion and false security. Only he can awaken us who is himself liberated from all illusion. He has been appointed by the Higher Government to be the focal point where the lifeline of the Eternal Music is flowing, drawing us to

the promised land. That divine Boatman is transmitting
freely the rapturous Music of the Shabd, the holy
Word, the sacred Naam. That Music will resound forever. The transmitter is one who is Word personified,
Word-made-flesh. He has been sent to pour over our
parched souls the life-enhancing Harmony of All-
Harmonies. It is the Music of the Spheres, the Comforter, the Voice of Silence. It is calling us to jump into
the Boat of Naam and sail to safety.

It is not enough to sympathize with the victims of
these floods; we have to give them practical help. Whatever we do for them is not enough, we must still do
more. But seeing their terrible plight we must also learn
a lesson: Life is far too short, too precious to waste;
from now on let us make the best use of every moment
that has been given to us. We should all take a vow never again to squander even a second but to be ever at the
door of the Beloved. He is so generous, so loving, so
forgiving. If we but turn our faces towards him in full
faith, he is willing to give us his spiritual treasures. If we
reach his door, we may be certain that he will ensure our
liberation from the constant round of transmigration.

Just as in the case of these flood waters where there
are eddies, whirlpools and dangerous creatures lying in
wait for us, riding on the spiritual waters there is many a
threat, many a hazard, many a disappointment. A
perfect Master is aware of every danger on the spiritual
way. He has overcome them himself. He can also steer
us through the stormiest sea and enable us to reach the
haven of safety, the haven of peace, the haven of
contentment which knows no change.

Come, let us now at least begin; let us now attend to

the warning voice of Nature and to the voices of those
who have suffered in the calamity of this flood. Let it be
a poignant warning to us to put "God first, and the
world next!" He who has a sensitive heart cannot but
listen to this warning voice. The Beloved's chosen ones
cannot ignore the Beloved's pleas any longer. How long
can we expect him to sing out the call to abandon our
shaky, unsound foothold on the shifting sands of
illusion and step into the divine Boat of Naam?

Yes, there are many who will be deaf, totally deaf to
this Celestial Music because they have entrenched themselves in lust, attachment and greed. They will be unable
to hear this Music. But a living embodiment of the holy
Word is perfect in heart himself, and can make anyone
who comes to him his own. Because of this great
capacity—the extent of which we are little aware—with
one glance of grace he can transform the most un-
worthy, the most hopeless into his own image. Spiritual
sensitivity is dormant in everyone; it is dormant like an
ember covered by ash. But when the wind blows on it,
once again it comes into its own, and glows with full
strength. And so we are, indeed, the divine Beloved's
chosen ones, for are we not like embers waiting for him
to blow upon us so that we may be ablaze with his
glory? It is only the ash of material illusion which has
covered the spiritual fire within us. And it is the law of
Nature that arranges an opportunity for the divine
teacher to come and blow away the ash which is smoth-
ering us.

The greater part of the life that has been given us,
the precious moments allotted us, have been squandered
in the graveyard of time. In the fleeting moments that

are left, it is incumbent upon us to redeem ourselves and turn them into eternity so as to win back the glory of the timeless. It is for us to use whatever time is left to reach the ultimate goal of human existence—the goal of self-knowledge and God-realization through contacting the unchanging permanence of Naam. The Master, through his glance of mercy and compassion, offers this boon, and by accepting it, salvation comes within our grasp.

CHAPTER SIX
THE
SAINT
AND THE
SCHOLAR

Kabir Sahib, along with Guru Nanak, came and blessed the people of India at a time when the political and social conditions in the country were far from satisfactory. During the 15th century the Hindus and the Muslims, who formed the major communities, were undergoing a period of great strife and struggle. Both religions had degenerated. The so-called religious heads—the maulvis, maulanas, and pundits—were not blessed with the gift of divinity. The knowledge they had was attained through the reading of books or scriptures, or from what was handed down by others. They had no inner vision of the Light of God or any experience of the Music of the Spheres. They had not solved the mystery of life and death themselves. To hide their own ignorance, they made the poor seekers after truth blindly follow rites and rituals which were the dominant feature of the day. Religion had ceased being a science whereby man could see God face to face through the grace of a living Master.

The so-called leaders were quite aware of their own

ignorance. They tried to make religion more and more complicated so that seekers after truth would become so lost that they would not ask searching questions about the origin of man, about God, and the way back to the Eternal Home. They hid behind a shield of verbosity. Since they could not explain spirituality in its true sense, they created a web of words to ensnare the poor seekers who came to them. Religion had become a profession, a trade. Both the pundits and the maulanas wanted to keep people busy in rites and rituals, from which they could make a lot of money and earn a good livelihood. They did not want anyone to probe into the real purpose of religion, or progress on the inner path.

At this juncture two religious movements began in India. Among the Hindus there was the Bhakti movement which based itself on love and devotion. It was itself divided into two further parts. One, headed by Kabir and Guru Nanak, believed in the worship of God in His original pristine glory which has no form. These saints believed that man has to rise above body-consciousness by sitting in meditation, traverse the higher planes, and ultimately merge in God Absolute, formless and without attributes. This is called the *Nirgun* branch of the Bhakti movement, and its exponents did not believe in performing rites and rituals. The other branch, called the *Sorgun* branch, believed God had attributes, and its exponents encouraged worshiping idols and pictures which symbolically represented God. This second school believed in the practice of rites and rituals which in time increased at a rapid pace.

The second great religious movement which arose

simultaneously among the Muslims is known as the Sufi movement. Sufism came as a reaction against the unlimited tyranny, unlimited oppression, unlimited cruelty of the Muslim kings over their subjects. The Muslim rulers did not want those persons who were really elevated, who had realized themselves and reached God, to have any sway over the people. They sought to promote Islam, but put only those in charge who were bigots and fanatics. Their religious counselors were in reality very narrow-minded; they were not open to conviction, and often ordered the persecution, and even the execution, of those who were following the right path. As a reaction against this tyranny, a sect of people who were sincerely interested in God, fled the cities and went into the wilderness. There they settled in small communities to meditate and pray. These people were called Sufis.

These parallel movements had already begun by the time Kabir Sahib and Guru Nanak came to bless this earth and put souls back in communion with God. Both, in their own way, taught the meaning and import of true religion. They not only taught the right principles, but were able to give a practical experience of rising above body-consciousness, contacting the Light and Music of God, and attaining the ultimate goal of communion with the Almighty. Guru Nanak presented his teachings in a very sweet, musical, heart-penetrating and persuasive manner. Kabir Sahib adopted a rather direct, instructive and sometimes pungent style. At that time many of the learned pundits presented their teachings in Sanskrit, and the maulanas gave theirs in Arabic, both of which were beyond the reach of the laymen. So Kabir Sahib began teaching in the local dialect. He was most loving and affectionate, but sometimes he used strong language when he wanted to emphasize the principles which had been polluted, especially when he was dealing with the ministers of both the Hindu and the Muslim faiths. He made it crystal clear when people were on the wrong path and were in wrong hands. He told them to beware of false leaders and follow the right path if they wished to achieve the ultimate goal of life.

The following hymn from Kabir records his conversation with a learned minister of Hinduism. This pundit, or learned man, claimed he had achieved perfect mastery of the scriptures. He had competed with the other pundits and had won all his debates, and began calling himself *Sarbjeet* which means literally, "winner of all." Unable to contain himself, he became an egotist and began boasting about his achievements and victories.

One day when he returned home he did not even pay his respects to his mother. She welcomed him, calling him by his first name. But since he was completely taken over by his ego, he said, "Mother, the entire world is calling me Sarbjeet, or victor over all. Why don't you also address me likewise?" The mother, who was a God-fearing woman, was very understanding. She realized that her son had gone astray, and wished him to come to the right path. She paused, and then said thoughtfully, "My dear son, I understand that there is a great saint by the name of Kabir. Go and discuss spirituality with him. If you gain a victory over him, I also will start addressing you as Sarbjeet." Sarbjeet immediately told her, "Mother, I will have an easy victory over him, and I will return in a few hours." So he loaded all his books and scriptures in a cart and proceeded towards the residence of Kabir Sahib, who was a weaver by profession.

The saints, of course, know what is in each man's heart, and Kabir immediately understood the purpose of Sarbjeet's visit. When the young pundit announced his arrival, Kabir came out of his house and received him with great love. Sarbjeet said, "I have come to discuss with you the interpretations of the holy scriptures. I have already defeated all the other learned pundits," and he named some of the famous ones of those days. Kabir Sahib said in all humility, "What is the hurry? Please have a seat. Take some food and then we will talk it over." Kabir served him to the utmost, but Sarbjeet was getting impatient to have the competition for which he had come. As soon as he had finished eating, he said, "Let us have one debate now." Kabir replied in all humility, "Oh, you are such a learned pundit. I am but an insignificant and unlettered man. How can I enter into competition with you? I agree to accept defeat without a debate." This was even easier than Sarbjeet had anticipated, and he was beside himself with joy. He told Kabir, "Please write down then that Sarbjeet has won and Kabir has been defeated." Kabir answered, "Write down whatever you want, and I will sign it."

So Sarbjeet wrote out the statement on a piece of paper and Kabir put his signature to it. The pundit then hurried back to his own residence. He was drunk with ego, and on reaching the house, instead of bowing to his mother or speaking to her respectfully, he just threw the paper down and said scornfully, "Look here, Mother, I have defeated your Kabir and here is the certificate! From now on, address me as Sarbjeet!" When the mother, who was a disciple of Kabir, picked up the paper and read it, she found that it said something quite different. Wanting not to be blunt and harsh with her son, she said, "Perhaps my eyes are not working properly, kindly read out what is written." When Sarbjeet looked at the paper, he rubbed his eyes once, twice, and yet again. Were his eyes deceiving him? He found the following words before him in his own hand: "Sarbjeet has been defeated and Kabir has won." How could such a thing have happened as he had written out the statement with his own hand! But, recovering himself, he said, "Mother, there seems to be some mix-up, some mistake in recording. But it doesn't matter, I'll go back and have it corrected."

And so the "all-conqueror" went back to Kabir, but this time his ego had come down a step or two and he said, "It appears, Sir, there was some mistake in writing out the previous statement. If you could sign a fresh certificate I would be obliged to you." Kabir smiled and said, "By all means. Write out whatever you want, and I'll sign it. But this time make sure you write the statement correctly." So Sarbjeet again wrote out on a piece of paper: "Sarbjeet has won and Kabir has been defeated," scanned what he had written, and the great saint signed his name. Reassured, the pundit returned home with his old air of superiority and handed the statement to his mother saying, "Here, I have got the requisite certificate and there is no mistake this time."

When the mother looked at the paper before her, she again found that it stated something else. So she told her son, "It appears that my eyes are still not working well; please make sure that whatever you are telling me has been precisely recorded." He said, "Mother, there is no possibility of any mistake, because this time I have not only written it in my own hand, but I made sure that what I wrote was correct. I reread it many times." The mother, however, insisted, "But you must read this statement to me before I can address you the way you want me to."

When Sarbjeet took the paper and read it, he was shocked to find once again the words: "Sarbjeet has been defeated, and Kabir has won." He became deeply agitated and began cursing himself. He thought, "Kabir gave me the chance to write this myself! What a fool I was to record it wrongly both times! I have never made such a mistake in all my life. Am I capable of committing such a blunder twice?" Troubled and somewhat humbled, he once again took his mother's leave to return to Kabir Sahib and sort out this strange mix-up. When he returned this time, Kabir was ready to perform a surgery and open Sarbjeet's eyes to the truth. So when he arrived and again requested the necessary certificate, Kabir Sahib responded with the words recorded in a famous poem. Kabir used simple, colloquial speech. Let me translate what he had to say:

> *My friend, how can you and I think alike?*
> *How can your path and my path be the same? I*
> *say everything on the basis of my personal ex-*
> *perience and you say everything on the basis of*

bookish learning. You do not even know that spirituality is a matter of personal experience; it is not a matter of intellect or inferences. Whatever I talk about I have seen with my own eyes. My inner vision is open with the grace of God, and what I say is based on direct experience. Whatever you say, either you have read from the scriptures or you have heard from other people; you have had no personal experience. The scriptures cannot be understood correctly unless you are properly guided by a living Master who has solved the mystery of life and death and who can help you to solve it.

Kabir Sahib is explaining that before one is initiated into the Mysteries of the Beyond, the words in the scriptures are like pillars of stone in a world of silence. They do not speak, and they do not convey their right import. They are merely an object of veneration for us. They are like Sleeping Beauties who do not talk to us. It is the magic touch of a living Master which bestows the gift of eloquence to the words in our scriptures. The moment they receive the magic touch of the living Prince of men, the silence of the words becomes eloquent. Each word of the scriptures begins to speak, and each line of the scriptures begins singing a melodious hymn. The words of the scriptures awaken from their age-old slumber and reveal their true meaning and significance.

Spirituality is not a path of blind belief; it is a path of seeing and believing. It is a path of faith, but one duly supported by one's own experience. It is a path

which goes to the extent of affirming: "Even if your
Master tells you something, do not believe it unless you
have experienced it for yourself."

*Whatever I say solves the problems of seekers
after truth. When they come to me I answer them
in a very simple way and in a few words, and all
their difficulties are solved. My words come
directly from the heart and they go and touch the
heart of the listener. On the contrary, you try to
confuse people, and make the confusion worse
confounded by taking cover under a shield of
verbosity, and by asking them to spend all their
time in the performance of rites and rituals
which have nothing to do with the esoteric side
of religion. You tell whosoever comes to you: Go
on reading the scriptures, and complete a
hundred and one recitations of the holy book;
Give so much money to the priest and so much in
alms; Go to the places of pilgrimage, into the icy
Himalayas, or the burning sands of Arabia; Do
penance for decades if you want your prayers to
be granted. As a minister you involve people in
such practices which become a source of income
to you. You and your like are exploiting religion
as a trade, as a means of livelihood. While giving
advice to people, your true object is to fleece
them as much as you can, and to hide your own
ignorance under verbiage. There is a world of
difference between your attitude to life and
mine.*

The saints always teach that the scriptures are meant

to be revered, not utilized for making money. We should earn our livelihood by the sweat of the brow and leave scriptures for something more sublime, something higher. The saints explain everything in simple words. Their teachings are shorn of any dogma. They do not take a single cent from their disciples. On the other hand, they distribute freely the treasures of divinity, the highest gifts of both the worlds. What a vast difference between the saints and our religious ministers.

I give a message of awakening to all the seekers: Awake, arise and do not stop until you reach your goal. I ask them to awaken from their slumber, but you teach them to remain in slumber. You give them opium of endless scriptural interpretations and superstitions.

I advise my friends to perform their worldly obligations, but to do so in a spirit of detachment. I bring all seekers after truth to the inner realms which are beyond the sphere of human attachment. On the other hand, you teach them to be more and more attached to this material world. You tell people that if they want wealth and the fulfillment of their desires, they should perform endless rites and rituals—which you are happy to superintend for them. You say if they want gold, they should first adorn your idols. You try to make them hungry for more and more wealth, for more and more power, and they become hopelessly attached to this world. When people come to me I explain the true significance of worldly riches, of worldly attainments and

titles, and of worldly relations. I emphasize that
everything in this world is ephemeral in nature,
transitory and short-lived.

Except for the gifts of the holy Word and the living
teacher, we depart from this world alone. Friends and
relations, position and wealth, often desert us during
our lifetime—during the various trials and tribulations
that we have to face. And even if they stay with us, at
the time of death none of these can accompany us to the
next world; they are all left here. Why should we be
attached to those things which cannot go with us to the
next world?

The saints teach us to live in the world in a detached
manner. They want us to be like the lotus flower which
has its roots in the muddy water but floats above it, or
the swan which lives in water, but can fly above with dry
wings whenever it desires. While living in the world we
should be in conscious contact with the Light of God
and with the Music of the Spheres, and never forget our
spiritual goal.

As I said earlier, Kabir was given to blunt and
forceful speech. We have now a rather memorable
example of the way in which he would illustrate his
points:

You are like a prostitute. How can you, who
have never had the opportunity to be one with a
true Beloved know the path of constancy and
love?

Spirituality is a path of having one overruling
passion: We should have one desire, one goal, one

longing—that of union with God. This is meant for those who never deviate from the attainment of their goal. It is not a path for those who bow their heads before every threshold or who crave for the fulfillment of every desire. And so Kabir told Sarbjeet:

> *Since you have not seen your Beloved, since you have not loved your Beloved, you go from place to place, from desire to desire, wasting your time. In the process you are losing your own chastity—you are losing the heavenly characteristics, the heavenly qualities, with which you were bestowed at the time of your birth. You are losing them one by one, and have come to such a pitiable state.*

Speaking of the true means for purifying ourself, Kabir says:

> *The various rivers, which are places of pilgrimage, can only clean the dust and dirt of our bodies; they cannot clean the sins from our soul. If we want to wash our sins away we have to go to the real river of purification which is the Water of Life—the Holy Word. It is only by bathing in the Naam or Word that we are rid of the dust and grime of mind and matter. Then our soul goes beyond the physical, the astral, and the causal planes, and reaches the stage where it realizes it is of the same essence as God.*

And having pointed out, one by one, their incompatibility, Kabir concluded:

*Look at the difference between your path and
my path. You waste your life in the attainment
of the transitory, whereas I utilize my time in the
attainment of the Supreme, the Eternal, the
Immortal.*

CHAPTER SEVEN
SCIENCE
OF
INNER RELAXATION

Meditation can help us not only in attaining inner communion with the Lord, but it can also help us in relieving the ailments which result from the stress and strain of daily living.

According to the Surat Shabd Yoga—the science of the soul—the basis of meditation is attention. *Surat* means attention itself. Meditation is based on focusing the attention at the center of the soul, the third eye or the single eye as stated in the scriptures, which is behind and between the two eyebrows. This practice leads to ever greater concentration, and we become increasingly oblivious to all the pains, tensions, and afflictions of life. During the process of meditation we enjoy perfect peace and perfect bliss.

This bliss which is attained through meditation adds an element of consciousness to our soul. It is said that God is an Ocean of All-consciousness; and our soul, being of the same essence of God, is also consciousness. Unfortunately, ever since the soul was separated from its source and imprisoned in the physical body, it has been lost in mind, matter and illusion. We all know that in this world everything is transitory, and most of the possessions and achievements that we take pride in are not lasting. We are constantly seeking happiness, but are unable to find it. The reason is that no amount of material comfort or material gain can give happiness to our soul which is a conscious entity. If we want peace and bliss for our soul, we have to give it the gift of consciousness.

Even with the progress of science, even with our marvelous material achievements, man is no happier today than he was before. Unless we progress in the domain of the spirit, our mind cannot be at rest, and unless it is at rest it cannot be relieved of tension and the ailments caused by stress. Saints and seers from the dawn of history have emphasized the necessity of developing greater and greater consciousness until we achieve cosmic consciousness. And we can attain cosmic consciousness only when we are able to concentrate at the eye-focus with single-minded attention.

At present our mind is in constant turmoil; it is worrying about one thing or the other. In order to be relieved of this worry and the tension it brings, we must learn how to concentrate our attention, which is said to be the outward expression of the soul. For this we must go to an adept in the realm of spirituality—the science of the soul. Spirituality is not a set of rites and rituals as it is popularly thought to be. This human body is the laboratory in which we can have ultimate communion with the Creator. Like all other sciences, this also has to be practiced under the guidance of an adept—a master of the science. When we want to perform an experiment in chemistry we go to a renowned professor in chemistry. If we get the right constituents and perform the experiment correctly under his personal guidance we are bound to get the correct results. Similarly, our soul as well as God both reside in the laboratory of the human body and it is only when we go to a living Master that we experience a direct link with divinity. When we go to a living Master he gives us, on the very first day of initiation, a direct link with the Light of God and the Music of the Spheres, the two expressions which God assumed when from the Formless He came into Form. Thereafter, by discipline we gradually develop both these gifts of the Lord.

For preparation of the ground, and to accelerate our progress on the path, saints have emphasized the need for living an ethical life. An ethical life provides us with the base for progressing on the spiritual path. One element of such a life consists of developing humility. Humility first, humility second and humility last can be the key to success in our lives, for unless we rid ourselves of ego and egotism we cannot be relieved of our tensions. Along with humility, we should develop a spirit of selfless service; that is, we should render service to the entire world without expecting anything in return. We should also lead a life of purity, a life of chastity, because "Blessed are the pure in heart for they shall see God." If we lead a pure life, then naturally we will be truthful: We will be honest with ourselves and with others. And if we are honest in the execution of the duties assigned to us, then the chances of developing worries and tensions are reduced. Along with these factors we must adopt nonviolence as our way of life:

noninjury to anyone, in thought, word, or deed.

If we combine all these factors in our life we will find that we become perfect men. All great saints and Masters taught the religion of man. They taught us to break the barriers of caste, color, creed and nationality. They taught us to have love and compassion for all mankind and for the entire creation. If we are able to develop this love, then all other attributes—all the heavenly attributes—shall be added unto us in due course.

Unless we become perfect men, unless we have a firm base of ethical values, we cannot overcome our tensions. We should try to perform our duties honestly and not encroach upon the rights of our fellow men or injure their feelings in any way. If we become true men, true citizens, we will radiate love and affection to all those who come in contact with us, and we will be automatically creating an atmosphere of harmony, of love and affection; an atmosphere free of the afflictions caused by tension. Love conquers all obstacles and beautifies everything that we encounter in life.

Once we have an ethical base which makes for harmony and peace in this world, we need a spiritual boost. This can come only from a living Master, for life comes from life and light comes from light. It is the personal touch and the personal guidance of the adept in this science which leads us into higher realms of spirituality.

The technique of meditation is to sit in a relaxed posture and concentrate our attention at the center behind and between the two eyes. While we concentrate, we mentally repeat a mantra. Those who are initiated

repeat the Five Names charged by the thought transference of the living Master. Those who are not, can
repeat some hymn or Godly names, or any name of
God, or the name of any prophet. If we sit for some
time we will be able to control our mind from roaming
about. Our tensions are created because we are not able
to control our mind, and it runs amuck. Sometimes we
think of one problem, sometimes of another problem,
and most of the time we are continually brooding. At
times we do think of those factors which are a real cause
of tension, but we are mostly afflicted with self-created
tensions. We often fear our own shadows in life, with
the result that we find ourselves in a very sorry plight,
and go about with a drooping face and are constantly
worried and agitated. But if we are able to control our
mind, if we are able to fix our attention at the center of
the soul, then we will not brood; we will be delivered
from self-created anxieties.

It is our attention which is the root of worry and also
of bliss. In our everyday life we find that when we are
sitting lost in thought, or are concentrating on solving a
problem or composing a poem, even if someone passes
by us or calls out to us, we may be quite unaware of it.
It is said that Isaac Newton was once solving a
mathematical problem and a band of musicians passed
by. After they were gone someone approached the
famous mathematician and asked, "Which way did the
band go?" And Newton, who had heard nothing,
replied, "What band? When did it come? When did it
go?" Who can escape hearing a whole band of
musicians? But Newton was so engrossed in his own
work that he was not aware of the band passing by. So it

is all a matter of attention. When we control our attention and focus it at the center of the soul, then we feel at peace. Our body is relaxed, our mind is relaxed and our spirit is relaxed. This is what is meant by sitting in meditation, and it relieves us of our anxieties, of our pains, of our afflictions, and it will afford us complete relaxation and bliss.

At the same time we become better men, and better citizens of the world. While performing our duties with honesty and truthfulness, we will also be increasing our output because of our greater concentration. We will be more efficient in whatever we do. If we are students we will master our lessons in a much shorter period than usual, because both learning a lesson and sitting in meditation involve the same process, which is one of concentration. By developing this gift of concentration of our attention we become more efficient workers. If we are able to work with single-minded attention, then even while working in the middle of a busy office, our output will increase. When we are not able to pay full attention to our work, our output falls. When our mind roams about, and is somewhere else, this naturally decreases our efficiency.

This science of inner relaxation is the way taught by the Masters of spirituality throughout the ages. They have laid the greatest emphasis on concentrating our attention at the eye-focus, because attention is the basis of meditation. By the process of meditation we become better students, better workers, better men, better citizens of the world and, side by side, we progress in the domain of the spirit as well! If we are able to focus our attention at the center of the soul, then we attain bliss. Even after reaching this stage, according to the saints we rise above body-consciousness and go into the higher regions. We enter those regions of complete consciousness, those regions which contain no material element, those regions which are beyond the sphere of tension.

CHAPTER EIGHT
BIRTHDAY
BEYOND TIME
AND
SPACE

Life is a journey interspersed with many a milestone marking its different stages. It takes time to move from one stage of life's journey to another, and through these milestones we can measure the distance we have traversed and the time we have spent in doing so.

The goal set before us by the Masters beckons us to a point beyond the limits of time and space. It beckons us to a destination, beyond this life, to a point which lies beyond the limits of this physical world. To realize the self and to merge with God is the ultimate objective of our life. To achieve this, we need to come to the feet of a perfect Master so that through his glance of grace we may transcend body-consciousness, merge with the radiant Master within, and under his guidance, traverse plane after plane until we enter Sach Khand. Thereafter, with the blessings of the Satguru, we can move forward until we finally merge into the Supreme Creator in His formless state.

If we complete the journey and reach our goal within a period of ten years, then in ten years we will have gone beyond the realm of time and space. If, through the special grace of the Satguru, we can cover the ground in five years, then in five years we will have gone beyond the restrictions of time and space. The saints and sages come to free us from the shackles of time, from the shackles of seconds and minutes, of hours and days, of weeks, months and years; all these categories of life are reduced to zero. Godmen come among us to release us from the bonds of time. They free us so completely that thereafter there is no need for milestones, no need of divisions to mark the distance we have covered. So long as we are caught in this world of illusion and attachment, we are subject to the restrictions of time and place. The saints are beyond all such limits. That is why it has been said: "They are beyond birth and death. It is to uplift mankind that they come, and by their life-impulse enable us to become united with the Lord." Having reached the ultimate goal in life, how can there be any further journey for them? How can time have meaning for them: time with its minutes, hours, days, months and years?

So when the saints come among us, it is only for our upliftment and salvation. Blessed are those who find their way to the feet of such holy ones, and blessed are those who saints call to themselves and who find a haven at their holy feet. In spite of our blemishes, our shortcomings, our enslavement to the world and worldly desires, the Master has taken us to himself. The Master belongs to the realm of immortality, and in taking us to himself he takes us within the ambit of eternity. Even in our wildest imagination, could we have hoped for greater blessings? Having been extended such infinite grace, is it not incumbent on us to make ourselves worthy of it? Is it not essential that step by step we strive on the way Homeward? For lives like ours, milestones are not enough to mark the stages. There have to be little stones to mark each yard, each furlong; and thus, step by step, furlong by furlong, mile by mile, we must wend our way.

You will find that on this journey, our pace bears little relationship to the pace of time. Time moves speedily; but we crawl at a very slow speed indeed. The result is that time passes by and we hardly make any progress in life's journey. Our aim should be that we not only move in step with time, but that we move faster than time, in order that we may reach our goal well before death knocks at our door.

This is the first principle we have to learn from the saints. If we have learned this supreme lesson, our life is indeed blessed. If not, of what use is this life, of what meaning the birthdays which we celebrate? Who knows how much time remains for us—how many years, how many days, how many moments? We are indeed uncertain about how much time we have left, yet when we look at ourselves we find that far from covering any substantial part of the way, we have not even traversed a few furlongs. We have a right to celebrate our birthday only when we have attained the goal of life—only when we have gone beyond the limits of time and space. But the truth is, we find ourselves chained to time, chained to space, chained to the different milestones of this long journey.

One of the enigmas of life is that even if we have some idea of the journey ahead—some idea of its extent—we have no idea of the time which is allowed us. I do not mean that we are absolutely clear about the different stages of the journey, but we do have some notion, some idea. When it comes to the length of our lives, however, which of us knows with any clarity, with any certainty, how long he has to live?

Man has reached the moon and is reaching out to the planets beyond. He has provided himself with every means of leisure and pleasure. In Chicago there is a very tall building called the Sears Tower. You can reach the 103rd floor within forty-five seconds. But such accomplishments deal with the physical body, the material world and its comforts. Such things bring no peace, no solace to the soul. We are spirit, an atom of the Ocean of All-consciousness we call God. What gives comfort to the body does not necessarily give peace and comfort to this atom of the Ocean of Consciousness. The saints come to teach us that peace and happiness are not to be found in the material world. They tell us this out of love; they often exhort us, and passionately, intensely, warn us against our mistakes. At other times they use the agency of suffering in order to teach us this lesson. One way or another they try to get across to us the secret of inner peace and happiness, but we are so obtuse that we refuse to learn.

This indeed is the tragedy of tragedies in our human existence. Is it not a simple, straightforward matter? Knowing the supreme grace which the living Master has bestowed on us, the grace which has disregarded our sins and limitations and which has given us the secret of immortality, then why this delay, this hesitation? Why leave things till tomorrow? Why even leave this important work till the later part of today? We should get going right away—here and now! We must not leave things till tomorrow, but must do them now; only then can we hope to attain salvation.

We light candles on birthday cakes—one for each year—ten, twenty, thirty.... As we blow them out, we seem to be full of joy and happiness. But what right have we to such rejoicing? He alone has a right to celebrate who has reached the goal of his life. Those of us who have not, those of us who have not even traversed the first furlongs, how can we think of celebrating the passage of the precious time that has been given us? If this is not illusion, what is? We are all caught up in this grand play of maya! We clap, we sing, "Happy Birthday to You"! To celebrate thus may be justified for him who has successfully moved from stage to stage, but for most of us, who are sinners and still far from our goal, such celebrations can only be a mockery!

A poet has compared the chimes of a clock to a bell that every hour tolls the knell of passing life. Let us take heed. Through the cycle of the seasons nature sends us due warning, but such is our folly that we do not attend to it. It is only those who have had the veil of illusion rent by coming to the feet of a liberated one, who learn to heed such warnings and move toward their goal. We need to respond to the countless warnings that life affords us so that we may make something of our existence. The path of forgetfulness, of forgetfulness in pleasure, is not ours to tread. We must not allow our consciousness to be suppressed under the burden of worldly pleasures. We must instead learn to pay heed to every beat of our heart, to every cry of the soul. Ours is the path of awakening, the path leading to the Eternal. It is for us to respond to the lightest heartbeat of every leaf, to learn from every object with which nature surrounds us.

Sant Kirpal Singh came to teach us this very lesson. He came to make us the subtlest of instruments so that we might learn to respond not merely to the beat of our own heart, but to the beat of the hearts scattered in all creation. Such was the degree of Sant Kirpal Singh's development even as a young man, that it is recorded that once when having a meal at his brother's, he had a stomachache. On experiencing this pain he questioned the source of the food they had eaten. His brother was compelled to admit that it had not been earned by the sweat of the brow. We too have to become so sensitive, so developed. Instead of the slumber in which we now find ourselves, we have to develop a kind of alertness, a subtlety, whereby we can respond to the slightest tremor, the faintest footfall of time. But instead, we slumber like Rip van Winkle, as though time did not exist, as though this life were never to pass away. Instead of making the most of every precious moment, we have become deaf to the footfall of time.

If time has any value, it has value because of us. If we can traverse life's journey in ten years, who benefits? It is we ourselves; for whatever time is left us, it will be a time of liberation, of bliss, of freedom. It will be a time of at-onement with the Lord, a time of infinite peace, a time which knows no sorrow and no pain, a time in which we live beyond the reach of ordinary joy and sorrow. We will no longer be subject to the sighs, the sufferings, the pangs, the anguish, which are inherent in

the normal human condition. As I have put it in one of
my verses:

I set out at the dawn of creation;
    now I am approaching its sunset.
Life is short, but the journey of love
    is long.

So each birthday is like a milestone. It is a point at
which we need to take stock of how far we have traveled
and of the time we have lost. We pride ourselves on our
wisdom and think there could be no wiser man than
ourselves. Yet we are willing to fight even for a trifle because we are full of vanity and ego. Have we ever
stopped to consider that even the commonest peddler is
wiser than we are? When the day comes to a close, a
peddler takes stock of what he has sold by the evening.
But do we stop to take stock of our losses and gains?
Every shopkeeper, every businessman, once a year has
his premises cleaned, redecorated; the windows and the
doors are opened in the hope that the Goddess of
Wealth will step in on the night of the Indian festival of
Diwali. But do we ever remember that we have to await
the coming of the Lord? Have we ever endeavored to
purify the soul, clean ourselves so we may be fit to receive the Beloved?

We talk a good deal, but do we ever really take stock
of our lives? Have we ever stopped to discover the
extent of dirt that we have collected, to find out what we
need to clear out in order to prepare for the arrival of
the Lord? Is our heart pure enough for receiving Him?
Are we always thinking of Him and yearning that He
may come? This heart which He has given us in sacred

trust, does it live by Him and for Him? If we have accomplished this we are blessed, and we have a right to celebrate our birthday. If we have not, instead of a day of celebration it becomes a point of warning, a warning against our wasting the precious moments that have been given us.

I grant that it is not easy to keep the heart perfectly pure. But if we make a sincere effort at least we can then tell the Beloved, as Muhammed Iqbal has said: "Behold the intensity of my desire; behold my capacity for awaiting Thee!" I grant, too, that we do not dwell in marble palaces or crystal palaces of glass. At best we live in houses of clay. But even clay houses need to be dusted, need to be repaved. Have we cleaned the huts which have been given us? Have we kept the doors and windows open? Have we sat in waiting to receive the Beloved? Have our eyes remained fixed on the entrance; have our eyes yearned for His coming? If so, our lives are fully blessed, our birthdays are blessed, and blessed will be the new year. If not, then such days are days of warning, days when we must take heed of where we are going.

We have been blessed in having been given human birth; and blessed in having come to the feet of a living Master, the soul's Beloved. The beloveds of this world sport with us only once in a while. But such is the infinite love of the soul's Beloved that if we only turn to him, he is happy to sport with us every moment of our lives. He is willing to take us beyond the limitations of time, through the realms within, to the Supreme Lord Himself. And thus, cradled in his divine love, we reach our ultimate destination. This destination is one of all intoxication, all concentration, all bliss and happiness, where there is no time, no space, no journey, no beginning and no end. This destination is the Ocean of All-consciousness, of love and of ecstasy, a state of being where there is no I-ness or thy-ness. There is no desire, no attachment, no ego or vanity, no hatred; there is only bliss, intoxication and love.

What more could we ask for? If in spite of this we fail to make anything of our lives, can we be forgiven? Can we, in that event, be permitted to celebrate days like this?

CHAPTER NINE
FINAL CHAPTER
OF
TRANSMIGRATION

Coming to the feet of the Master is the final chapter of the long epic of the soul's countless births and deaths in the physical world. We think that the moment we come to the Master's feet, our life will become trouble-free and filled with the quintessence of ecstasy and all the gifts of God on earth. We think that by coming to the Master's feet we should be relieved of all sickness, all poverty, all ignominy. But this is a misconception. Every thought, word, and deed has its corresponding reaction, and we have to deal with the heavy load of karma resulting from deeds committed both in the past and during our present life. The Master's job is to see that our karmas are wound up in this life, that we are cleansed and purified so that he can take us to our Eternal Home. He wants us to complete the final chapter of the book of our life so we can proceed on our way to communion with God.

This heavy load we are carrying consists of three types of karmas. First, we have the *sanchit* or storehouse karmas, those which we have been accumulating throughout our various lives since the painful story of the separation of our soul from God began. Our deeds have been heaped together in the karmic storehouse, pile after pile, hill after hill, mountain after mountain; it is beyond human ken. Because we cannot ourselves liquidate them, the Master, at the time of initiation, takes away all the sanchit karmas.

The second type of karma is the *pralabdh* or fate karma which has been allotted to us for this life. These are the fruits of our past actions which we must bear in this lifetime, and which account for our present condition. These have to be undergone in this life. Nevertheless, even this karma is reduced to a great extent by the grace of the Master. He dilutes it as a chemist dilutes a solution. If, according to our karmas, we were to be sentenced to go to the gallows, the Master can reduce that sentence to a pinprick. Sometimes, if we are due to undergo a serious illness, we have only a minor one. Many of the karmas we were to suffer are eliminated by the Master, while others we go through in a milder form. He can even make us undergo some of our pralabdh karmas more intensely during a shorter period of time, or less intensely over a longer period of time.

The disciple does not realize that in spirituality and mysticism, it is said that physical suffering, poverty and ignominy are blessings that are sometimes bestowed on a disciple even though the disciple is not in a position to appreciate their purpose. Hazur Baba Sawan Singh Ji used to say that whenever one of these boons befalls us we should consider ourselves blessed because we are in the process of being purged.

When we are healthy, when our life is going on all right, when our children are well fed, when our business is prospering, and when we command all the benefits and gifts of God on earth, then most of us are likely to forget God altogether and become lost in the gifts. But if we find that our body is not in very good health, or our business is not prospering, we begin to look to God for help. Generally, it is when we start suffering a little that we start remembering God. And we seek His indulgence to come to our rescue. When we are in affluent circumstances, then our tendency is not to think of God. So if illness, or poverty, or ignominy can turn us to God, then in this respect, they are said to be blessings.

Also, these three boons help us to purify our character. First they teach us gratitude. We are so callous that we rarely feel grateful to God. One of the greatest failings of man is his habit of exploiting everything to the greatest possible extent. We always crave for more and more, and pray for more and more, but we forget our basic obligation and duty: that we owe our gratitude to God for whatever is given to us.

Then again, when we pass through a period of prosperity and good health, and when we are at the zenith of our reputation, we become a little pampered and pompous; we scoff at others. Instead of becoming humble, we become egoists and sometimes go to the extent of becoming egotists. But when we are sick, we are shorn of this ego. Sickness brings us to the lowest ebb of our existence and then we develop sympathy for those who are also in that state. When we become ill, if we have not previously prayed from our heart of hearts, we will begin praying to God. When we ourselves suffer, we begin having sympathy for others who are in physical agony. When you are sick yourself, you know what it is like to be sick. A man who has never been sick will be indifferent or critical of those who are sick. But when you are in the throes of a terrible plight, you start praying for others as you pray for yourself. We develop humility and sympathy for all around us. That is why the Masters sometimes allow their disciples to undergo these karmic sufferings.

The same is true when we experience poverty. There is a Persian proverb which says that in poverty even your shadow abandons you. Our relations and friends are faithful so long as we are prosperous. But when we undergo a prolonged period of poverty, when all our hopes are dashed to the ground, everyone leaves us and we begin withdrawing our attention from the world and start directing our attention within. And what is spirituality? It is the path of inversion.

When we experience ignominy, when our reputation is marred, we lose the sympathy of those around us on whom we count. Howsoever we may profess that we believe only in the support of God, if we look within ourself, we find that we do not depend on His support alone. In reality we depend on the flattery of our admirers and on the goodwill of our relations and friends. We think that if we are in trouble, they will always come to our rescue. But when they fail us and we are bereft of the goodwill and sympathy of those around us, then our attention converges, and is focused on the Master, on God. Then we make fast progress on the spiritual path.

Besides the sanchit and pralabdh karmas, there is a third type of karma known as *kriyaman* or daily karma which we are creating during this life for our future. Man is not entirely bound by fate or predestination. He has been given a zone of twenty-five percent where he has free will, in which he can incur further actions and reactions. Seventy-five percent of the events in our lives are due to reactions of our past karmas and are considered predestined, but we do have some free choice and can perform either good or bad deeds. We may think that performing good actions will lead us to salvation, but this is not so. Lord Krishna has said that good actions are as binding as bad actions. Our good deeds and our bad deeds are like chains of gold and chains of iron—both are binding. As long as we remain in the first three worlds—the physical, astral and causal planes—we are bound by the reactions of all our actions. The law of action and reaction is upheld by the Negative Power, called Kal, who is in control of these three regions. He has established regions of heavens and hells for the rewarding and punishing of souls according to their karmas. After death, each soul is judged by the Lord of Judgment, known in India as Dharam Raj. If the person's good deeds have a predominance over his bad deeds, he is sent to paradise or heaven for a specific period of time. If the bad deeds outweigh the good, he is sent to hell for a certain length of time. The mystics speak of still a third region, *ahraf*, an area intervening between heaven and hell. If there is a balance of good and evil deeds, a soul is sent for some time to ahraf. After the allotted time is spent in heaven, hell or ahraf, the soul is again sent back for another life. The performance of good actions alone will not lead to salvation, for according to the karmic law we must continue in the cycle of rebirth in order to reap the rewards of our deeds. Thus on our own, we are incapable of finishing off these karmas by ourself. We cannot render our karmas ineffective. How then can we end this cycle of returning again and again to the various species of lives?

The only escape from the wheel of transmigration is to come under the protection of a perfect living Master who is capable of nullifying these karmas by giving us a contact with the Light and Sound of God—the Naam or Word. Those who are thus blessed transcend the karmic chains, whether of iron or gold. A Master is able to take us beyond the limits of the first three worlds to the fourth stage—Bhanwar Gupha, where our soul sheds the shackles of mind, matter and illusion. The karmic accounts of souls who are initiated and thus come under the protective wings of a perfect Master, are taken over by him.

The Masters say that someone with a strong willpower, duly supported by the Master's grace and guidance can avoid creating new karmas. Given our twenty-five percent area of free will, we are liable to keep adding to our karmic burden of actions and reactions. But if we make a sustained effort to follow the Master's commandments and cease to be the doers, we can reduce by five or ten percent, or even more, this area in which we create new karmas. In fact, if we surrender ourself fully to the divine Will, our kriyaman karmas are reduced to zero. If we utilize properly the area of free will by leading an ethical life, devoting time to our meditation, and doing selfless service, we can save ourself from creating new karmas for which we would have had to bear the fruit. In this regard, the self-introspection diary devised by Sant Kirpal Singh is one way we can weed out our failings so we do not incur future karmas.

A living Master helps us to bring to a close the final chapter in the epic of transmigration through which our soul has been passing. First, at the time of initiation the sanchit karmas are taken over by the Master completely. Then, the Master intercedes so that the pralabdh karmas are undergone by the disciple in a watered-down form. Next, the Master gives the disciple guidance and instructions on how to lead a spiritual life so that he incurs no further karmas. Ultimately, if the disciple learns to rise above body-consciousness, he receives the Master's boon of intoxication, bliss and joy, and in that state of ecstasy, he passes through the pain, suffering and turmoil of his remaining karmas, unaffected by them. In this way, a disciple can proceed joyfully on his journey to union with the Creator.

CHAPTER TEN
ETERNAL SPOUSE

As I was coming up the staircase leading to this hall, I was struck by an atmosphere of hilarity, of joy and jubilation. On inquiring, I was told that it was on account of a marriage party. I thought this encounter very appropriate, for I myself was coming to this assembly where we have gathered in order to attain divine wedlock. The prime purpose of our meeting together is to find out how we too can arrange for our marriage, for our nuptials with God, the Eternal Spouse.

Everyone is in search of everlasting bliss, everlasting peace, everlasting intoxication and ecstasy. But we have not yet been able to attain our heart's desire. The great mystic poet of Persia, Maulana Rumi, has depicted the condition of the soul as it dwells here on the earth plane. In the opening of his *Masnavi*—known as the Koran of the Persian language—he says:

> *Listen to the absorbing tune of the flute,*
> *and understand the tale it is relating;*
> *in reality it is telling the story of*
> *separation—the separation of the soul*
> *from God.*

I thought we should consider the story of the soul's separation from its Creator, and see how we can end the longing, the pining, the pain, the affliction which it suffers as a consequence.

All scriptures agree that God is love; our soul being of the same essence as God is also love; and the way back to God is through love. It is the story of love, the story of the longing of the lover to be reunited with the Beloved—and it is told in all mystic literature. Such literature is full of descriptions of the pain and yearning of the soul for reunion with the Oversoul. And when this wedlock is achieved, the bliss attained is beyond words and not subject to time. As Mira Bai has said:

> Blessed is Mira, the Lord is her Spouse.
> As He knows no death,
> she knows no sorrow.

The basic concept in mysticism is that we are all brides, irrespective of whether we are male or female, and there is only one spouse, the Eternal Spouse, which is God. According to the mystics, it is not until the bride weds the supreme Bridegroom, that she ends the story of her tragic separation and attains immortality. We are all waiting for the auspicious moment to arrive when the bonds of our nuptial relationship can be forged, when we can be bound together in everlasting wedlock with our Eternal Spouse. Even in this world, the bride and the bridegroom are always pining and longing for that moment when they can attain their union. The melodious strains of an orchestra at an Indian wedding represent the approach of the bridegroom who is eager to catch sight of the beloved. Traditionally, as the bridegroom approaches, the music of the orchestra becomes louder and louder, and the tempo becomes faster and faster, symbolizing the ever-increasing beats of the heart of the bridegroom. Until the moment of union comes, the beloved likewise is full of intense yearning.

In the code of spirituality, the greater the intensity of our feeling of separation, the quicker we can bring about the fulfillment of our desire to be one with our Eternal Spouse.

Since meditation is the means by which we can meet our Beloved, the Masters advise that when we sit for meditation, we should remember our Beloved from the core of our heart. We should experience the pangs of separation—not just talk about them, but actually experience them. For this reason, saints, seers and Masters ask us to chant or read, before we meditate, a moving hymn which expresses an intense desire to be with the Beloved, which expresses detachment from worldly affairs and which speaks of an overriding desire for union with the Eternal Spouse. When we approach our Beloved through meditation we have to think of only one object, we have to remember only one, and we have to contemplate on the form of only one, to the exclusion of everything else.

Meditation is a path of constancy, of single-minded devotion. But what generally happens when we sit for meditation is we think of many people, many places, and many things at the same time. The result is that we either do not achieve our prime object in life or, at any rate, we are delayed for a very long time from achieving it. If we choose to be one with the Divine Beloved, then the first thing we have to do on the spiritual path is to settle our priorities. Sant Kirpal Singh, after matriculating or graduating from high school, had to make a decision as to what he should do in life and what should be the order of his priorities. After many days of inner debate he came to the decision: "God first and the world afterwards." And because he never went back on this decision, he achieved his goal. If we also make the same decision, then we will consider our union with the Beloved as priority number one in our life. We will attend to our worldly duties and obligations in a spirit of detachment. If we are able to achieve such a state of mind, then surely the day will not be far off when we are able to unite with our Beloved.

Speaking of his own Master, Bhai Nand Lal Goya said: "One life-inspiring glance of yours is sufficient to enable us to attain our objective in life." We too can attain union with the Eternal Spouse through the benign guidance of a living Master who bestows upon us the gift of the Holy Word. In Sufi mysticism, a living Master is known as the divine Cupbearer. He is one who intoxicates us with his lyrical glances, who inebriates us with his ecstasy-producing wine.

In the terminology of the Sufis and of the Urdu and Persian poets, the word "wine" refers to the wine of spirituality. It does not refer to the ordinary wine produced from grapes. The intoxication induced by physical wine is completely gone after three or four hours. But the wine of the Word of God, the wine of the love of God, is so ecstasy-producing that its effects never lessen, and anyone who tastes it, is intoxicated for all time.

There is a story from the life of Guru Nanak which illustrates this. When Babar, the founder of the Moghul Empire, became Emperor of India, he put many a saint into jail. In prison, Guru Nanak was allotted the work of grinding wheat with a hand mill. When Babar's chieftains went to the prison, they found, to their astonishment, that Guru Nanak was busy praying and the mill was working of its own accord! They reported to Babar: "Nanak seems to be a man of God. He is busy praying, and the mill grinds on its own." Afraid that the great saint might put a curse on him, Babar invited him to the court. When Guru Nanak arrived, Babar proffered a cup of hashish saying, "We are brothers; let us sit down and share this." But Guru Nanak politely refused, saying, "O Babar, this cup of yours intoxicates only for a while, but the wine of Naam, the Eternal Word, which I drink, intoxicates forever."

Such indeed is the difference between the wine pressed from grapes, and that of Naam bestowed on us by the Master. The divine Cupbearer makes us drunk with the love of our Eternal Spouse by giving us a single draught, by affording us a conscious contact with the Primeval Light and Sound of God on the day of initiation. He bestows the cup of immortality on us at the very first meeting. As I have said in one of my verses:

> Love is the beginning and end of both
>   the worlds;
> And I have brought this immortal gift
>   to be bestowed on all.

In this ephemeral world where all things have but a

short life, it is the love of God alone which makes for immortality. The divine Cupbearers bestow this gift of eternal love—and they bestow it with utter abandon, pouring out their pitchers of divine love to all.

When the Masters come into this world they do not come for any particular society, any particular country; they come for humanity at large. They have themselves become immortal, and they bestow immortality on those who come in contact with them. First, they teach us to lead an ethical life, because a life of purity is the basis of spiritual progress. Sant Kirpal Singh Ji used to say, "It is difficult to become a Man; but once one becomes a Man in the true sense, it is not so difficult to find God." They teach us the religion of Man. The Masters do not interfere with existing religions. They tell us: If one is a Christian, he should be a true Christian; if a Sikh, he should be a true Sikh; if a Moslem, then he should be a true Moslem. We can remain within the fold of our religion and our society, but we should strive for union with our Eternal Beloved.

A living Master can help us attain our heart's true desire. He can make all the arrangements for our wedlock with God. By the living impulse of his attention, by his lyrical glances he enables us to rise above body-consciousness. He opens our inner eye and we see the Light of God and, rising higher, merge in the radiant form of the Master. After that, he guides us through the higher planes until we at last reach the supreme stage in spirituality—the stage where nuptials of the soul with the Eternal Spouse take place. That is the point where the drop merges with the ocean and becomes the ocean, the ray of light merges with the sun and becomes the sun. And thus united with the Beloved, we become self-oblivious and forget all about our little selves. We attain eternal bliss, eternal peace, and eternal jubilation.

This is how we can bring the tragic story of our separation to an end and restore the bride-soul to her immortal Bridegroom—the Eternal Spouse.

CHAPTER ELEVEN
PREDICAMENT
OF
MAN

Khwaja Hafiz paints a vivid picture of the strange ways of God and of man's unenviable predicament:

Man has been tied hand and foot to
a plank
And tossed on a stormy sea with the
injunction that he must not allow a
drop of water to wet his garments.

Such is the Persian mystic's complaint against God's justice, such is the nature of our condition. Indeed, we have been tied to a plank and abandoned on the high sea. Our helplessness is indeed pitiable. The soul yearns to be united with its Creator, but however much it endeavors, it seems to be unable to make even the least progress.

These words of Hafiz embody the cry of the soul. Man finds himself helpless on the stormy waves of the world and yet is required, as he floats among them, not to allow even a drop of worldliness to soil his garments. How difficult, how impossible, to fulfill such a commandment! We are all caught in the web of illusion, enslaved to the senses and the mind. The soul has become so identified with the mind that it does not even recognize itself. It thinks of itself as the body, not independent of it. As the Hindu Shastras put it:

The need for food and sleep, and the
desires of the flesh, tie us to the
body through a thousand temptations.

The cause of our enslavement is the mind which is always in search of pleasure and indulgence. It is always tempted to simultaneously seek all the pleasures of this world, and is never satisfied with any of them. Such is the state of our delusion in this world. Our senses draw us to the world outside. If the eye beholds a beautiful object we are attracted to it. But the physical beauty that we see, the beauty of the human body, the beauty of flowers, trees, rivers and mountains, is not the true beauty. It is only ephemeral. Real beauty resides within; it is that infinite principle which is at the heart of each and every object of creation.

Sant Kirpal Singh used to say that even if one of our senses becomes dominant, it is sufficient to destroy us. The moth is dominated by the sense of sight and is drawn to the flame. When it sees the candlelight it flies into the flame and is destroyed. The deer is the fastest, freest of animals, and is swift enough to fly from the leopard and the tiger. But upon hearing the drum it is relentlessly drawn to it, and allows itself to become a captive, spending the rest of its days in the confines of a zoo or a private garden. The fish falls an easy prey to its palate. It may roam the river at will, but when the angler casts his baited hook, it unsuspectingly swallows the bait, and pays with its life.

Each of our senses is a source of great temptation. One of the mightiest creatures is the elephant. It is so massive and powerful, it can uproot trees. Yet, it has one weakness—it is blind in the pursuit of its lust. Those who wish to trap him dig a large pit and cover it with twigs, branches and loose earth. After they have camouflaged the pit, they erect a large effigy of a she-elephant. When the male is overcome with desire for his counterpart he rushes towards her and falls headlong into the pit. Unable to escape, he is left there for days, until through hunger, he is tamed and finally domesticated. As sexual desire is to the elephant, the sense of smell is to the *bhanvra*, a type of bee. It can bore through the hardest of wood, and yet its love of fragrance causes it to be entrapped in a flower and die. Citing these examples, Sant Kirpal Singh would explain that if even a single sense can lead the most powerful creatures to slavery and death, how vulnerable then is man, in whom all the senses are highly developed?

Khwaja Hafiz in his verses is making an impassioned plea to God. He is drawing attention to the countless temptations to which man is subject, and to the impossibility of God's injunction that man keep himself free from the soiling touch of this world. Anyone who has stood by the sea and watched the great waves lashing the shore at high tide, knows how such waves can wash over and pull down anything. Caught on such waters, is it possible for anyone to escape their spray, to remain dry in their midst? Hazrat Shamim Karhani, the Urdu poet, has said:

*On the one hand our Maker demands that
we adhere to the path of righteousness,
And on the other hand He has beset the
way with every possible temptation.*

As we live out our lives, as we tread the way, we are
constantly dogged with the fear of slipping and falling
into temptation. Strange indeed are God's ways; strange
the paradox of life. We are promised immortality if we
can keep to the right path, and yet at every step we are
subject to desires and temptations. Caught in this
paradox we are reduced to a state of helplessness.
However hard we labor, however sincerely we yearn to
return to our Creator, we are compelled to realize our
own helplessness, the impossibility of our situation.

When a soul realizes the impossibility of its plight, it
cries out to the Lord to ask Him why He has condemned
it to such a predicament. How, it questions, in the midst
of so many whirlpools and snares, in the midst of such
sweeping tidal waves can it keep itself dry? As it realizes
its own helplessness, its own incapability to protect
itself and keep itself dry, the protest turns into a prayer.
The soul turns to its Creator for help, for without Him
it can accomplish nothing. Its own strength cannot lead
it to salvation. There is only one way, one answer to its
problem—the assistance and refuge of the Lord. It
prays to Him to come to its rescue and save it from
certain destruction. God alone can protect it and keep
its garments dry. And when such a cry for succor issues
from the depth of our being, God cannot but hear it.
Guru Gobind Singh has said that the Lord, before He
listens to the trumpeting of the elephant, hears the cry
of the ant if that cry issues from its heart.

Realizing its helplessness, the soul cries out to the Lord: "I have tried everything, I have strained my strength to the utmost, but to no avail. I have sought to pursue the path of good actions. I have read the scriptures and performed various rites and rituals. I have fasted, and I have been on pilgrimages. But though I have done all this, I find myself helpless and unable to return to You. I cannot even take one step towards the goal which lies within. My friends, relatives and neighbors are of no avail, for the moment I am faced by a strong temptation I am helpless. Its high waves sweep over me and engulf me. I have not spared any efforts; I have worked hard and with sincerity. And yet for all this, I am unable to move forward by even an inch. Lord, unless You come to my aid, unless You protect and succor me, I am nothing."

When this cry bursts from the soul, God hears it and heeds it. Once this yearning to be united with God has filled our heart, we are in perpetual anguish, in perpetual realization of our helplessness. The Lord cannot but heed this call of the anguished soul and move to answer it.

When we surrender ourselves completely to His protection, accepting our vulnerability, He takes charge of us. Taking the rags of the human body, He comes down among us to help us return to our Home. The Arabic word for God, "Khuda," literally means, "He who comes on His own." God Himself does come in the form of saints—Godmen. They come on their own for our salvation. They are embodiments of the Absolute, the Supreme Father. They are human mouthpieces of the Lord.

Strange indeed are the ways of God. He may come
and dwell among us, eat and drink with us, and play
with us. But unless He Himself gives us the vision, we
are unable to recognize Him. In one of my early verses I
have said:

> *I see in this human frame the glory*
> *of God;*
> *And yet I am puzzled, for this glory*
> *is unperceived.*

That is why when the saints and Masters come
amidst us, not many recognize them. What a paradox
that the Supreme Creator, the Lord of this world and
the next, comes and dwells amongst us, and none but
those to whom he bequeaths the requisite sensitivity can
recognize Him. It is for this reason that the Sufis say
that love first emanates from the heart of the Beloved.
Unless the Master takes compassion on us and fills us
with love, we cannot come to his feet. Many are those
who behold them, but it is only a few to whom he re-
veals his true greatness.

Even when an official visits our area, we stand forth
and salute him. When the governor, the prime minister
or the president comes our way, the whole world is there
to greet and applaud him. And yet when the Supreme
Creator walks among us, He can pass by without any of
us recognizing Him. As Jesus once said to his disciples:
"Have I been so long time with you, and yet hast thou
not known me . . . I am in the Father and the Father
is in me." But man is not really to blame for this
inability to see. By himself he is helpless. "Some hearts
are reserved for the play of love; that music cannot be

played on every instrument." It is only the blessed few on whom the Lord has mercy and casts His glance of grace, who have the power to perceive Him. The rest of the world proceeds unseeing on its unhappy ways. "O Nanak, those eyes are different with which one sees the Lord."

We have been separated from our Father since time immemorial. Through the grace of the Lord we can at last become one with Him and bring to an end our age-old pains, our age-old anguish, our age-old yearning.

It is now for us to make the best use of the human birth we have been given. We read and hear the words of the saints, but how many of us really live up to their teachings? We may understand what they say and agree with it, but it is so hard to live by what they say. When we go to a funeral we are confronted with death. For the moments that we are there we recognize the inevitability of death and are moved by it. But such is the force of worldly relationships, that once we return home we forget and become lost in our worldly ways. Likewise, when we go to a saint and hear the eternal wisdom, however moved we may be at the time, we fail to live and act by it. We go home and act as though we are totally ignorant of our ultimate goal and of our obligation to pursue it. It is not enough to read about spirituality. It is not enough to understand what the saints say. What is needed is that we translate it into our daily life, that we live by what they teach us.

What a great blessing that, seeing the helplessness of man, the Lord should come among us and bestow His riches upon us. It is now for us to take mercy upon ourselves by following His commandments. By doing so and reshaping our life, we can reap the reward and return to our Home. What helplessness was ours, what frustration! There seemed to be no answer, no help, no protection, no refuge. But the Lord called us to Himself. If we could recognize even a fraction of what God has done for us, we would be filled with such infinite gratitude that we would live by His commandments, overcome all our temptations, and reach the shore with not a drop on our garments.

CHAPTER TWELVE
PREDICAMENT
OF
GOD

Maulana Rumi has said, "God made man to play the game of love with Himself." All prophets and scriptures describing creation have said that in the beginning God was alone in an eternal state of bliss, ecstasy and peace. All souls, which were really particles of the Oversoul, were in a latent state—united with Him, deeply submerged in Him. Some mystics say that God became tired of this uniform existence, of this loneliness, and He had a wish for variety. He thought He needed someone to love Him. So He said, "Let me separate souls from myself and send them away for a while so that when they return they will be bubbling with the intensity of love." Unless there is separation, an intensity of longing is not created. If two people remain united for a long time it becomes routine, and in due course, the warmth of feeling dwindles. So the game of love, of necessity, began with a little separation.

It is said that there was a vibration and a flutter and the Lord assumed two forms: One was the Music of the

Spheres and the other was the divine Light. The Muslim scriptures use the phrase "Kun-Fia-Kun," meaning, "God said 'Be' and it became." First one soul separated from Him. Then He muttered to Himself, "Mischief, thou art afoot." When He got an inkling of how wonderful it was to become a Beloved, He created more and more lovers. Those lovers were the souls which were separated from Him. The more the lovers, the more enchanted became God's life. He started enjoying being the Beloved and having a number of lovers around Him. As this game was extended He found that He was adored more and more, He was loved more and more. He was the object of enchantment, the object of beauty. Because He enjoyed this game He decided to extend it. First a plane of all-consciousness, Sach Khand or Muqam-e-Haq, was formed. Thereafter another plane was formed in which there was only a little illusion mixed in with consciousness. Then a third plane was formed in which consciousness and illusion were equal. Another plane was then formed in which illusion was slightly more than consciousness. Next a plane was formed in which illusion predominated and consciousness was in the minority. After these planes were brought into being, so many more universes were created. At first the souls who assumed the human body merged directly in God when they left the physical form. This describes the game of love, the beginning of the story of separation, created by God. Because He was tired of the same endless ecstasy and bliss, and because He wanted some fun and frolic, God became the first infidel in love. Had this practice continued, all the separated souls would have returned to God after only a short period of time. They would have rushed back to Him with a great passion and zeal. But somehow that mischievous game started by Him became prolonged, spelling doom for the souls and also putting God into hot water. Instead of this being the conclusion of a short story with a happy ending, it was only the conclusion of the first part of the monumental epic of separation, full of pathos, yearning, pining and agony.

It is said that God created the Negative Power to control the causal, astral and physical planes of creation. The Negative Power has its own job to do—to keep these worlds populated and running properly. Electrical power is the same everywhere, but it can be used to freeze or heat. Similarly, the Power of God is always the same, but when it goes out into expression, away from its Source, it is called the Negative Power, and when it returns to its Source it is called the Positive Power. It is said that the Negative Power underwent a long period of meditation and penance, and as a reward for his austerities, he asked the Supreme Power for three boons, which God in His own wisdom granted. The first boon was that when the soul left the human body it should not immediately return and merge in God. The second boon was that the embodied soul should not remember anything of its origin or of its past lives. The third boon was that if God wanted any soul to merge in Him, God should assume the human form and take the soul back through the medium of satsang or discourses alone and not by showing any miracles. The Negative Power feared that if God assumed the human form and performed miracles, in a short time his entire kingdom would be desolate and all the souls would return to God.

In the beginning God thought He would be a silent spectator, watching the souls shedding poignant tears due to separation from Him. But He forgot that all these souls were the same essence as Himself. He had made man in His own image. Man is a micro-God— God on a miniature scale—who has the same attributes as his Creator. Man said, "If God out of mischief can subject His own creation to suffering and cruelty, then we can subject Him to a counter-blast. We accept God's verdict, but if we must writhe in pain and flutter our wings in complete helplessness, then we will not allow God to enjoy this sight as a spectator from a distance. We will pull Him down from His heavenly seat to the earth-earthy plane to suffer along with us." Thus, man, by voicing his grievances in all sincerity and with great force, brings God down from the pinnacles of heavenly glory, from the limitless heights, to the barren and scorching earth. Man cries, "I am suffering in this land. Since I am bearing the torture of this physical body, You too will have to adopt the painful burden of the physical form." God cannot help but respond to these cries, and thus, man brings God down from immortal and ineffable heights to the scorching sands of the earthly desert. God comes here and works through a human pole; He burns His feet and moves amongst us with painful blisters, paying heavily for the sporting game devised by Him for fun.

In order to wind up His own game, He had to begin coming to the earth to take man back to his Eternal Home. The human pole which God works on is called by different names: Master, Guru, Christ, Saint,

Prophet, or Messiah. Through the process of initiation, the Master gives the soul a contact with the inner Light and Music of the Spheres, the primal manifestations of God. Then, under the guidance of the Master, the soul ultimately reunites with God and brings to a close the story of separation. The Masters don the human attire, this filthy and frail human body, and come to live among us. They befriend us, love us, and by radiation, entice us to love them in return. They inspire us to engage in earnest in the game of love. Through this process they embrace us, take us out of the mud and mire, and clean us so that we can rise above body-consciousness and become one with our Creator. They bestow their grace with their lyrical glances, and create a bridge through which divine and godly attributes can flow into us. We then begin to imbibe the highest spiritual qualities and begin leading an ethical life.

We have no idea of the love and affection that God, working through the form of the Master, bestows on us to convert our poor, base metal into sublime and precious gold. We have no conception of how much He suffers to do so. We do not experience even an iota of the suffering and labor the Master undergoes. We have no realization of what the Master does for us. Masters take pity on the earth-earthy souls who have been separated from their Source for trillions and trillions of years. They take on the karmas of all those who have been initiated by them. They are so compassionate that they save their disciples from untold pain and torture. Since they are the embodiments of love on earth, and since love knows only selfless sacrifice, they willingly take on the karmas of so many people and provide them with relief from their actions and reactions. Because the Masters have merged in the Ocean of All-consciousness, and become one with God, they have no karmas of their own. They are not bound by the laws governing the wheel of life and death. They receive their commissions directly from God. They come to this earth at will and also leave the earth at will. So the law of action and reaction is not applicable to them. But when they take on the karmas of others, naturally those karmas become their own. And according to the laws of nature, they undergo some physical hardship.

We think only we are suffering and that God is having an easy time, but this is not the case. The Masters always undergo tremendous suffering, for they take upon themselves much of the karmic burden of their disciples and have to undergo mental anguish or physical pain. How can the disciples know how much of their karmas the Master takes upon himself, and how much he suffers? A disciple sees something of the sacrifice only when a Master is crucified, beheaded or flayed alive. Yet in response to all aggression and tyranny the saints only give love. They are like the fruit-laden tree which gives ripe fruit even to those who strike it with a stone. If you study the lives of the saints you will find they sacrifice themselves on the altar of love. The Master undergoes so much suffering for us, silently and unperceived. With the naked eye we cannot see even an iota of what torture the Master undergoes for us, unappreciated and unsung. And even when a Master is put on the cross, beheaded or flayed alive, there is hardly a disciple who will admit that the Master underwent it for his sake.

We often talk about the pain on the path of love, the pining, the longing and the anguish of love. But when we receive the fruits of this path, imagine how much pain we are rid of and how much bliss becomes ours. Have we ever thought of the torture and pain we have to undergo when we pass through the cycle of transmigration, through the 8.4 million species of life? After one cycle of birth and death ends, another cycle starts; and when that cycle ends, yet another one starts. Have we ever thought of comparing the agony we undergo while passing through this process of transmigration to the pain involved in our treading the path back to God?

I have often been asked: Since God is all powerful, why doesn't He simply say, "I am going to do away with the game I created with its pains and fires and take the separated souls back at once"? To understand why God does not do that, let me relate to you an incident from the Indian epic called the *Ramayana*. It is said that in ancient times Dasaratha of Ayodhya was an ideal ruler, being strong, noble and compassionate. He had four wives and from the eldest was born Lord Rama. His youngest wife, Kaikeyi, gave birth to a son named Bharat.

During those times wars were fought with chariots. Once when the king was in the midst of a battle, the axle joining the two wheels of his chariot broke. His youngest queen, Kaikeyi, stretched out her hand and let the wheel turn on it, keeping the chariot moving, and enabling the king to win the battle. In appreciation for her service he granted her one boon which she could ask for at any time.

Years rolled by and the time came when Rama,

being the eldest son, was to be declared as the heir apparent. The entire kingdom loved Rama and rejoiced when that announcement was made. Even Kaikeyi was happy about this until her maidservant said to her, "Why are you so happy? Tomorrow the eldest queen's son will be heir apparent and the king's appreciation for you will dwindle." Hearing this, the ape in Kaikeyi got the better of the angel in her. She determined to make use of that boon promised to her by the king. She wanted her own son, Bharat, to be king and wanted Rama sent in exile for fourteen years. Kaikeyi threw off her bangles and ornaments and when King Dasaratha returned to the palace he found his wife distraught and in a miserable plight. Her hair was disheveled, and her eyes were full of tears. He never expected anything like this. When he asked her what was wrong she told him her story of woe, vented her feelings, and asked for the fulfillment of the boon. She said she wished for her son, Bharat, to be heir apparent, and for Rama to be exiled. The king was taken aback. Rama was not only loved by the king, but he was the cynosure of the whole family as well as the entire kingdom. So the king refused to grant her that boon.

When Rama came to know about the boon his father had promised Kaikeyi he went to the king and said, "Revered Father, you are a kshatriya (a member of the warrior class), and a kshatriya's word must always come true. He has to keep his word even at the cost of his life." So the king agreed to be true to his word and fulfill the promise he had made to Kaikeyi. Rama thus had to leave the kingdom, and his faithful wife, Sita, and his brother Lakshman, accompanied him. Bharat also loved Rama dearly, and when he found out what had happened he refused to accept the kingdom for himself. He ran after Rama and begged him to come back. But Rama said, "No, my father has given his word and I have to see that it is honored."

Similarly, God is also bound by the promise He gave to the Negative Power. God is caught in His predicament. He is bound by the terms of this contract. Yet God is so gracious. Man is in a prison house undergoing a life sentence, undergoing atrocities and tortures. But God sends the benevolent Masters to come to release man from that prison and save him from third degree methods and beatings. If someone releases you from bondage, naturally you have love for that person.

Hafiz has said:

> *Talk of the Supreme Musician and the*
> *Divine Wine, and do not try to delve*
> *into the secrets of the world;*
> *Nobody has ever been able to reveal them,*
> *and nobody will ever reveal them*
> *through philosophy.*

Rather than delving into the secrets of how this world came into being, and why God created this game, it is high time we started singing of the beauties and the exquisite music of the Cupbearer, the Divine Musician. People have been asking these questions since the dawn of eternity. Nobody has yet found the solution, nor are they likely to find one. These questions are asked from the intellectual level, but when we cross the third region we transcend our intellect. When we enter the purely spiritual realms, there is no intellect. There are no hands, there are no feet. It is a realm where we walk without feet, where we work without hands, and we speak without tongue. The saints put a stop to intellectual questioning by saying, "Why not first reach the presence of God! You can then ask Him these questions yourself." But when you reach God, when you merge in Him and become one with Him, who will there be to ask questions, and from whom will come the reply?

PART II

CRUCIBLE

CHAPTER THIRTEEN
DIVINE BEAUTICIAN

In order to progress on the spiritual path, we need to develop right understanding so we can have right thoughts, right words and right deeds. Unless we lead a life which is pure, which is moral, how can we expect to rise above body-consciousness, see our Beloved within, talk to him inside, and journey into the higher realms? In order to get a boost into the beyond we first need a base, and all Masters have taught that an ethical life is that base.

Each day we have so many shortcomings in leading an ethical life. We have so many failures in the areas of nonviolence, truthfulness, chastity, humility, selfless service, maintenance of a strictly vegetarian diet and avoidance of drugs and alcohol. If we count our daily failings in these areas, take a pen and mark a spot on our face for each of them, and then we look in a mirror, we can see the face we present to the Lord when we go to meet Him. Do we want our Beloved to see us in this condition? A bride puts on her best clothes and tries to emit the most luscious fragrance before going to meet her bridegroom. She cleans off all the blemishes, all the spots on her face. She wants to appear before him as an ideal beauty. Similarly, if we are going to meet our Eternal Beloved within, we will want to first rid ourselves of our scars and blemishes and appear with a clean, shining, resplendent face. We want our face to be beaming with beauty, beaming with grace, beaming with compassion.

Unfortunately we have developed ugly blemishes and are covered with the dirt and dust of the sins we have accumulated while passing through the wheel of transmigration. How many times have we gone wrong in matters of nonviolence? We injure the feelings of so many people, we think ill of so many others, and we are even violent to some. And because of our grievous lack of patience, we are prone to speak harshly. Just count how many scars and blemishes we put on our face each day because of lapses in the area of nonviolence alone!

In matters of truthfulness, how many lies do we tell during the day? How many times do we deceive, even cheat others? How many times do we encroach upon the rights of others? All these are failings which mar our countenance.

The saints always teach "humility first, humility second, and humility last," but how many times a day do we fail to be humble? Humility means treating every human being as our equal, and speaking to each one in a humble tone, with a sweet voice. But we find that we only know how to speak humbly and with a sweet tongue to those who are superior to us in material wealth or material power. When we speak to our equals, we try to show off. And when we speak to our subordinates, or those who are in a lower position, our very tone smacks of ego. To how many people who are seemingly below us in wealth or position are we really sweet? We put so many spots on our face because of our ego: ego based on knowledge, wealth and power. We try to flaunt our knowledge. We try to overawe others with our power, and we try to prove our superiority to others on the basis of the riches we possess. How many of us really treat others as our equals, as brothers and sisters in the same universal Father?

Then, we lack compassion. When God made man He bestowed on him one quality which the angels lacked—compassion for his fellow beings. Man was created to have sympathy for his fellow beings, to share the pain, the trials and tribulations of others. We should share the sorrows and afflictions of our fellows, as well as of the entire creation. But instead we kill so many creatures to satisfy our carnal appetites, or for sport. In everyday life we see so many of our neighbors suffering. We seldom care if our neighbor is dying of starvation or of some illness. When we are driving on the road and see an accident, we seldom care to come to the rescue of the injured one, take him to the hospital and serve him. Just count how many opportunities for selfless service we do not take advantage of. As Etienne De Grellet has said, "I expect to pass this way but once; any good therefore that I can do, or any kindness that I can show to any fellow creature, let me do it now. Let me not defer or neglect it, for I shall not pass this way again." How many of us keep such a thought in mind as we walk through life?

We go wrong in the matter of purity, of chastity;

how many of us are chaste in thought, word and deed?
How many of us can pass the alluring beauties of this
world and yet remain pure at heart?

After counting how many dark spots we accumulate
each day, we begin to feel it is impossible to clean our
face of this dross—each moment our mind is engaged in
thinking, speaking or performing actions, the reactions
of which go to make new impressions, new scars. Thus
we go on creating more all the time. As a result, our soul
must continue coming again and again, without hope of
returning to its Source. How can we regain the beauty
required to enter into the court of God?

The only way to become purified is to show our scar-
laden face to the Divine Beautician—the living Master.
He is all compassion and is bound to have mercy on us
and help us remove our scars. Being in the company of a
living Master is in reality being in a beauty clinic. Just as
we go to a beauty salon for the removal of our physical
blemishes, we go to the Divine Beautician, the Master,
for the removal of the dark spots of our sins. He has his
own special techniques, he has his own special
cosmetics, and he treats us with the lotion of divine
love. With this lotion he removes the blemishes of our
sins, of our evil thoughts.

A beauty clinic has a special cosmetic for one kind
of blemish, and another for a different type of blemish.
It has various treatments for scars on the face, the arms
and other parts of the body. Similarly, the Master also
has different treatments for each one of our ailments.
He has lotions of nonviolence, lotions of purity, lotions
of compassion. But if we hide our ailments, how can he
treat us? Honesty is what is wanted. Only if we are

honest enough to allow our ugly spots to be seen, without camouflaging them, will we evoke the compassion of the Divine Beautician.

The Eternal Beloved is eager to meet us; he is also pining for the lover. But on this path the Beloved has a precondition—the absence of any scars or blemishes on our face. He is keeping a constant watch on us. The moment our face is spotless, and is sanctified by nonviolence, glorified by humility, illumined by truthfulness, and transfigured by chastity and selfless service, our Beloved will rush to embrace us. He is yearning and longing to come and bestow His love on us.

CHAPTER FOURTEEN
THE
MIRROR

If we read the biographies of great people we find that man has been trying to learn from his mistakes. When he becomes aware of his wrong actions, he tries not to repeat those failings. All saints and Masters have spoken of the necessity of overcoming the negative qualities in us and rising above our human weaknesses. Khwaja Hafiz, the Persian mystic, kept a big earthen pitcher by his side, and whenever he did something wrong he would drop a small pebble into it. After a few days he would be horrified to see that the pitcher was full.

Similarly, in India some of the sages of old kept a pitcher by their side and threw small grains into it every time they had a failure in leading the spiritual life. They discovered that within a short time the pitcher would overflow, revealing to them the extent of their weaknesses. Still others have taken account of their failings by putting a knot in their clothes. In the evening they could find out how many wrongs they had committed by counting the number of knots they had tied.

St. Ignatius Loyola, the great Christian saint,
prescribed that man examine his faults daily. First, he
said we should ask God for the grace to be able to
remember how many times we commit a particular
fault. Then, we should count how many times we
committed that fault during the day, ask pardon for it,
and determine to guard against that failing the next day.

This method of correcting our faults has been
developed in a very scientific way by Sant Kirpal Singh.
He created a daily self-introspection diary. This diary
lists the days of the month and has columns to note the
number of times we fail to observe, in thought, word
and deed, the ethical virtues. The diary form has
columns for nonviolence, truthfulness, chastity,
humility, selfless service, adherence to a strict
vegetarian diet (avoiding meat, fish, fowl and eggs,
both fertile and infertile), and avoidance of liquor and
intoxicating drugs. There is also a column to mark
down the daily time spent in the two meditation
practices of bhajan and simran.

If we fill in this diary every night, taking a realistic
view of our failings during the course of the day, we will
have a day-to-day record of our performance. We will
be able to see where we stand in our spiritual progress.
For example, if we have ten chances in the day to be
humble and succeed only in eight, we mark down the
number two to show we have had two failures. The
diary reflects those chances where we miss acting up to
the highest ideals—not the times we were able to act
correctly. This is known as negative marking. The
reason we mark our failures rather than our successes is
that a record of our successes will not present us with

anything we can correct—it will only serve to boost our ego. If we find we have failed a hundred times in one day, we will make every effort to reduce it to eighty times the next day, seventy times the following day, and less on succeeding days. Suppose for example, that today I had five chances to perform selfless service, and I wasted all five chances. When I see at night that I have wasted these opportunities, that stimulates the will to try to avail of such opportunities whenever they come in the future. Self-introspection leads us to the realization of our faults so we can try to set things right.

Our diary is a mirror we look at each night, so we can discover how many blemishes we have. As we are trying to prepare the best possible face in order to meet our Beloved, we want to remove all dirt and all scars from our countenance. This mirror of the diary shows us that we have failed so many times in leading an ethical life. And if we have accumulated so many blemishes, how can we think we will be presentable to our Beloved?

Once we become alive to our own dark spots, then we are more apt to reform ourselves and not spend all our time trying to reform others. It is our ego that causes us to see the faults in others and ignore our own. Swami Ram Tirtha once placed an advertisement in the newspaper which read, "Wanted, reformers—not of others, but of themselves."

The trouble with us is that we always try to pick holes in the characters of others. We spend all our time finding fault with others, but we never take even a minute to look into our own heart and find out what blemishes are in our character. Paltu Sahib has said that

if you want salvation you should stop thinking about
the ills of others, and start looking into your own heart.
And Christ has said, "Why beholdest thou the mote
that is in thy brother's eye, but considerest not the beam
that is in thine own eye?"

One of my verses is:

> *Those who are mad in love with thee, have*
> *no time to laugh at the affairs of others,*
> *They only laugh at themselves.*

If we are lost in the love of our Beloved, we will not
laugh at others, we will not have time to criticize others,
we will only laugh at our own blemishes and
wrongdoings. We are always very keen to have a ren-
dezvous with our Beloved. If we learn that he is coming
to our house, what do we do? We set our own house in
order. If I find my house is dirty and everything is
topsy-turvy, do I look with a telescope to see if there is
dirt and dust in a house fifty miles away? No, I sweep
out the dust and prepare a clean house for his coming.
Because of our ego we think we achieve the acme of
perfection in whatever we do and believe that whatever
others attempt to do is all wrong. When we see how
many of our own shortcomings are reflected in the
mirror of the diary, how will we then have the heart to
look at the failings of others? Our immediate concern
will be to get rid of our own faults, to beautify our own
faces.

If we are aware of the fact that we must fill out our
diary in the living presence of our Beloved, and if we
realize God's omnipresence, we will not only be more
conscious of our actions during the day, but we will also

be more honest in evaluating our failings. Seeing our condition, we will sincerely cry out for help to overcome our failings. And our Beloved will certainly respond and wash off the dirt of our faults. Then, when we look in the mirror of our diary we will no longer see ourselves reflected there, but instead will see only the Beloved.

CHAPTER FIFTEEN
MESSAGE
OF
FALL

Fall is the season when the leaves make their grand finale, bedecked in the brilliant attire of reds, oranges and golds, and exit leaving the stage bare for the cold and bleak winter. Unless the old leaves fall, how will the new leaves of life grow? It is fall which prepares the way for the entrance of spring.

Nature is a great teacher, and during this season it gives us the message of fall. Nature teaches us that we should give up our old ways and adopt new ones. The cold winds that pierce our bodies remind us of what pain, what damage we have caused to the hearts of our fellow beings. Autumn reminds us that our old habits should fall away from us like dried-up leaves, and we should blossom forth with the spirit of spring and rejuvenation. Like the gentle breezes of Zephyrus we should emit waves of warmth for our fellow beings. Nature's message is that the time has come for us to give up our callousness and develop compassion, love and sensitivity for every living being in creation.

One of my verses reads:

O fearless tipplers, have some regard
for the goblets and the cups,
When you tread through the world
of hearts, please pass carefully
and with gentle footsteps.

On the path of love we have to walk with great sensitivity, with great caution, so we do not trample on the delicate hearts of other living beings. This care that we take not to injure others is called *ahimsa* or non-violence. If we criticize other people in our minds, injure their feelings in thought, or wish them harm, these are failures in nonviolence in thought. If instead of applying balm on lacerated hearts, our words open up wounds or add salt to them, we have failed to follow the path of nonviolence in word. And if we strike someone or kill any living creature, that is a failure in nonviolence in deed.

If we analyze why we criticize and hurt others we find it stems from our ego. If we are filled with our own sense of importance and superiority, that is a lack of humility. But if added to that we also wish harm to another person, that is a failure in nonviolence. If someone is going on a trip for recreation and relaxation, and we feel that we should be the ones going instead, we may wish that circumstances arise so that he cannot go. That is a failure in nonviolence in thought.

To remain truly nonviolent, when we speak we should not interfere with things with which we are not concerned. Such interference is considered an indirect act of aggression. For example, if two people are arguing about something with which we are not primarily concerned, but we enter the fray by saying something, the result is that we get either a prompt rebuff or somebody is hurt by our interference. If we get a rebuff, we usually make a counter rebuff—and that is aggression. If we take one man's side and thereby make the other man's case weaker, that is also a type of aggression, because it is encroaching on somebody else's territory.

In the realm of nonviolence, it is not only what we say, but how we say it. We should keep in mind that it is out of the abundance of the heart that a man speaks. If a person who is full of jealousy or anger speaks, it appears that he is not uttering words but that he is letting loose scorpions which sting the listeners and injure their feelings. Our words should not inject resentfulness in the listeners nor denigrate them from the position they are occupying. A person who is upset is in search of soothing words, but if he instead hears critical and harsh words he will be more irritated and restless. Instead of our words causing his mind to become concentrated and at peace, they cause him to send out restless waves in all directions. And these waves often become storms which can induce in him a state of mind bordering on lunacy. When we speak, we should utter only those words which soothe the hearts of those listening, which ennoble and elevate their spirits, which permeate their very being and help them know themselves and know God. If hearts are bubbling with love for our Master and for God, and we have love and compassion for the entire creation, then whatever we utter will be full of love. If God's love permeates every pore of our being, then those who come in contact with us, those who listen to our words, those who are in tune with our vibrations, will benefit.

People sometimes ask me what they should do when they are surrounded by those who cause them mental worry, and are negative and irritating. What generally happens is that when somebody irritates us, we feel agitated. The result of our agitation is that if we do not resort to physical force, we end up abusing them verbally, or we wish them ill.

Instead of responding violently, there are several other things we should do. First, we should remain calm and quiet. If a person is obnoxious to us, instead of confronting him, we can withdraw from that person. But withdrawing from this possible confrontation should not be accompanied by our abusing the person in thought. If instead of wishing him ill we have loving thoughts and simply wish that person would stop irritating us, then we have entered the realm of prayer.

There are also times when we might want to have a sincere talk with the person who is causing us mental worry—but we have to be very cautious about doing this. We can have a heart-to-heart talk with some people, but if we have to deal with a touchy person, or a very explosive person, then we should use all possible precaution so we do not give him any cause to fly into a rage. Just as we dispatch glass goods in a box stamped with the words "Fragile: handle with care," similarly, we should handle fragile hearts and fragile temperaments with utmost caution. Experience is the best teacher. If we develop sensitivity, we will know how to talk to those around us so as to soothe rather than break or inflame their hearts.

But why should we be affected at all by the

negativity of others? Why should we tremble when we see a person approaching us—even if he has been negative towards us in the past? We should be so centered in the Master's love, so filled with divine intoxication that we remain unaffected. Those who have contact with the Eternal Word should be stronger than others. Whoever comes to us, no matter how negative they might be, should be influenced by our higher character. We should inject them with our own positive influence. Why should we fear the negative influence of others? Why should we have this phobia? Some people have a phobia of water, some have a phobia of heights. Why should we have a phobia of the negative feelings of others? Why should we suffer from an inferiority complex? Our faith should be stronger. Instead of being affected by others, we should radiate more powerful waves of love. We should emit the fragrance of love to everyone we meet. A Persian proverb says that if someone enters a perfume shop, even if he does not purchase anything, he leaves the shop carrying with him the fragrance. Why shouldn't our heart be such a shop which emits fragrance to all who come in contact with us? When we meet people, we should be able to ignite in our hearts the fire of love which has grown dim with the dark coverings of mind and matter. We should bring into full bloom our dormant qualities of immortality. Eternal Wine should flow through our eyes, and all who meet us should share in the divine intoxication. The beauty of this path is that those who are mad in love with the divine Cupbearer are so absorbed in ecstasy, they do not have time to criticize anyone, and they cannot be affected by anyone.

Why should we find fault and injure the feelings of others? Whenever we begin to have a bad thought toward someone, if we immediately think of the source of all love, if we think of the Master, all thoughts of violence and injury will vanish. In this way, we can transform our thinking, and by doing so, transform our lives.

We can change our old ways of thinking and living and adopt new ones. This is the message of fall. It is nature's message of hope and renewal. Now is the time to allow our old habit of injuring others to fall away from us like dead leaves. Now is the time to begin treading the path of love with a new, dynamic zeal and passion, showering kind thoughts, words and deeds on those around us. Now is the time for the rebirth of spring.

CHAPTER SIXTEEN
TRUE COLORS

Shakespeare has described this world as a stage where men and women are actors; they have their own entrances and they have their own exits. In the field of dramatics an actor consciously fools others. He knows that his own identity is separate from the role he is playing, yet he goes on stage and plays the part of Brutus in "Julius Caesar," or the part of Orlando in "As You Like It." He can play a role with which he has not even the slightest possible connection. He uses all his acquired skills so that it appears that it is not an act, but is reality. If he is a really good actor he can earn his livelihood as a professional, and can build up his ego by virtue of this accomplishment.

In our own lives, we who are not in the field of dramatics behave as actors. We act out parts or assume roles which have no relevance or connection with what we really are. We do this either to impress others and thereby inflate our ego, or to make a profession out of the pious roles we play.

The saints do not want us to wear hypocritical garbs,

neither do they want us to make a profession out of the spiritual teachings. Yet despite their exhortations, every morning we prepare a face to meet other faces; we do not reveal ourselves in our true colors. If we would review our life for one day alone—from dawn until late at night—we would see how many faces we assume. We would see how many dramatic talents and techniques we use, and discover what object we have in mind for each one. Our main purpose is to avoid showing our true self to anyone; we wish to delude other people and get what we desire out of them by our crafty means. Our whole life has become a camouflage.

The first thing we must learn is to reveal ourselves in our true colors to the best of our ability. In order to do this, we have to honestly introspect our thoughts, words and deeds. Spirituality is a path of truthfulness, and if we wish to progress on this path, we must learn to weed out untruthfulness from our lives.

There are three broad aspects of being untruthful: hypocrisy, falsehood and deceit. The difference between these is subtle.

Hypocrisy is the effort we make to conceal what we really are. If we honestly look into our hearts, we will realize that we commit sins in every sphere of life. We have all the ills in us to which man is susceptible. We lack purity; we do not have piety; we do not avail ourselves of even one percent of the many chances for selfless service which come to us. We are not humble, and when we talk, we always speak like a big boss. But because we have a lot of ego in our hearts we try to present ourselves as being spiritually advanced. We try to make people think that we are in tune with the

Almighty.

In our lives we assume many faces, and change those faces many times a day. For our family we put on one face. When we go to the office we put on another face. When we go to a social gathering we put on a third face, and at a political meeting we wear still another face. Our purpose is to avoid, under any circumstance, revealing ourselves in our true colors. We do this because we have so many failings and we want to cover up those failings and present ourselves in the best possible manner. Hypocrisy means that we are not sincere to others. We profess one thing but we practice just the reverse of it.

In any office, there are some people who do not work, but who stand and render advice to others to work hard, to be devoted to their jobs and to be punctual. But they themselves are neither punctual nor devoted to their work. This is hypocrisy.

If we are in business and use unfair means to earn more and more wealth, then we should not put on a false front and act as if we are the most pious people in the world. We may deduct unfairly a certain percentage from the pay of the workers under us, and out of that money spend part of it for charity. Then when people say, "Oh, he is a very religious man; he has made such a big donation," we do not tell anyone who really paid for it. This is not revealing ourselves in our true colors; it is also hypocrisy.

We put on a show and try to make others think we are honest, compassionate and humble, but in reality these qualities are conspicuous by their absence from our lives. We try to present ourselves as embodiments of the greatest divine virtues, whereas under the garb of our hypocrisy we practice all the devilish wiles. We think that if other people believe we are saints, they will respect us more and we will be able to have our own way. We should not try to create the impression that we are angels when we are not.

If we count how many lies we tell during the day we will discover how often we engage in "falsehood," which is the second aspect of failure in truthfulness. There are so many examples of how we tell lies. Suppose we are an officer in a department and a superior asks us to give an assessment of the work that we have done. Instead of presenting exact figures, we report exaggerated figures so that it appears we have done more work. If we are a businessman and a buyer comes to us, we often tell him, "Oh, I am not making any money on this transaction, I am just creating goodwill. For the time being, I am running my business on a 'no profit—no loss' basis." Or we say, "I am only taking two percent or five percent profit," when we are actually making more. This is falsehood.

Similarly, if our wife or husband asks us what our program is for the day, although we might be planning to go to the movies, we give the reply, "I have no special program—I will return home straight from work." We seldom tell our real plans to anyone—neither to our friends nor to members of our family. We are not even forthright with our Master! When the Master asks us about our progress in meditation, we say, "It is all right, Sir," even though in reality we have been neither keeping the diary nor sitting in meditation.

We are not honest with our children either. We tell

them, "You must do your schoolwork, you must stand first in your class." But when they ask us, "What was your position when you were at school?" we will reply with a chuckle, "Oh, I always used to stand first." We often ask our children to be more disciplined and to behave themselves, and naturally they ask us, "How did *you* behave in school?" We generally say, "I was a perfect example of discipline." This again is falsehood.

There are so many examples of falsehood in our lives. Sometimes a relation asks us in the morning to contact someone to do a job before we return home, but we forget to do it. Because we are afraid of having a conflict, we will say, "Oh yes, I tried very hard to contact that man. I tried to call on the telephone, and then I had my secretary call, but the man was not available." Or if someone asks us to purchase something and we forget to do it, we say, "That particular item is out of stock and the shopkeeper is expecting a delivery from the manufacturer within a few days."

If we arrive late at our office and are caught, we do not tell our boss that the reason we were late was we were talking with a friend and forgot all about the time. Instead we may say, "Somebody was seriously ill and I went to check up on him in the hospital."

Even though many of the lies we tell are innocuous, they are lies all the same, and lies come under the heading "falsehood."

The third aspect of untruthfulness is "deceit." One type of deceit is when we appear to be kind to someone, and under the veil of goodness we take advantage of him. We all deceive our friends, our relations and our acquaintances. We may advise a friend, "This is a good bargain." In reality, however, we have a vested interest in the sale. We may encourage another friend to sell his car or his house, and say, "I'll help you out; I am already involved in this type of business." While protesting that we are acting in a selfless manner as a friend, we proceed to take a commission on the sale. We lead others to believe we are trying to help them, when in reality we are trying to exploit them. This type of action comes under the heading of "deceit."

When we have been able to deceive others we are elated. But the worst part is that we ultimately deceive ourselves. Instead of recognizing our failings and weeding them out, we begin to revel in them. We are unwilling to accept that we have failings, and so we delude ourselves into thinking we are perfect. Then we try to present ourselves as the ideal man or woman on earth. If we can begin to realize and accept the fact that we are not perfect, and if we do not hide from others the fact that we have faults, then we can eliminate many of our failures in deceit, falsehood and hypocrisy. We can always succeed in fooling a few people, but in the final analysis, when we are untruthful we are only fooling ourselves.

CHAPTER SEVENTEEN
NEW DEFINITIONS
OF
LOVE

Myriads of saints and seers have sung of God in a variety of ways, but none have been able to fully define Him. Myriads can continue singing God's praises and still no one will be able to describe Him in all His facets. Since God is love, love cannot be fully defined either. We have hundreds of definitions of love, and even if hundreds more are sung by the saints and poets, love will still remain undefined. Generally, people believe that love consists of gazing into each other's eyes, but recently I came across a thought-provoking quotation by the French writer Antoine Saint-Exupery. He says, "Love does not consist in gazing into each other's eyes, but in looking together in the same direction." That direction is their ultimate goal. But in the realm of love between the Master and the disciple, love *does* consist of looking into each other's eyes. When the disciple is fortunate enough to receive the lyrical glances of the Master, his soul soars into the higher planes. Although seemingly paradoxical, both definitions of love are correct.

A disciple will make progress by leaps and bounds if he gazes into the eyes of the Master and thus attains a stage where he becomes completely lost in the Beloved. When a disciple looks into the eyes of the Master, he is looking into the eyes of the fountainhead of all ecstasy, all purity, and all virtue. When a bridge is built from the Master's heart to the disciple's heart, then naturally the divine attributes of the Master start flowing into the disciple, and in due course permeate his very being. It is only when the disciple becomes completely lost in the Beloved that he really begins his journey Homewards, rises above body-consciousness and learns to die while living. So the concept of gazing into each other's eyes is most appropriate when it relates to the love between a Master and a disciple.

Saint-Exupery said that love *does not* consist of gazing into each other's eyes. This applies to the relationship between one disciple and another. Those two disciples can be life-partners or they can be two disciples on the same path. The love between them consists of looking in the same direction, and that direction is the Master, is God. Gazing into the eyes of one who has not reached the highest realm of spiritual love, might lead to pitfalls. Disciples are, after all, disciples—they are not yet perfect and are still prone to weaknesses.

There is a world of difference between love and lust. Love takes you to the heavens, and lust takes you to the marshy lands of the earth. True love is chaste and leads us to the higher planes and communion with God. What we commonly call love in the worldly sphere is actually lust, and that leads us into a swamp. Lust entangles us in the mud and pulls us down. Both true love and worldly love give their own intoxication, but the results are vastly different. True love, chaste love, gives a lasting intoxication and ecstasy which makes us soar to spiritual heights. Worldly love or lust gives a temporary intoxication, a temporary carnal enjoyment, and it leads us into the swamp of sensuality. Once we fall into the quagmire we cannot escape unless someone comes to our rescue. If we remain in that pit we drown, and thus cause our own destruction. Divine love is constructive and leads us upwards, while lust and sex lead us downwards.

The way to attain true love is to invert our attention from outside, from the senses, and tap inside through meditation. When we begin drinking from the fountain of the Water of Life, and enjoy the inner celestial Sound Current, we are filled with ecstasy. That Water or Wine of Life has a far greater intoxication than physical pleasures. There is no comparison between the bliss which comes from meditation, and the temporary enjoyment which comes from sensual indulgence. Hazur Baba Sawan Singh would tell us that the mind is a lover of enjoyments. Having only tasted the enjoyments of outer music, outer beauty, outer fragrance, outer touch and outer taste, it has become lost in them. But once we invert, experience the music, the beauty, the nectar and the love of God which await us within, the mind finds that ecstasy so great it naturally gives up the outer pleasures. Chastity then comes as a by-product of our becoming absorbed in something much higher, much more sublime than the outer pleasures.

The best way to develop true love, or mystic love, is

for a disciple to look into the eyes of the Master. When we gaze into the Master's eyes we imbibe spiritual radiation from him, because he is the center of all grace and all divinity. When someone looks into the Master's eyes he is looking into something heavenly, something celestial, something which is all perfection. Through the Master's eyes we can catch a glimpse of the unchanging permanence. And when the Master looks into our eyes we are infused with a grace which lifts our soul to heights above our physical body and speeds us to our True Home.

Instead of two disciples looking into each other's eyes, they should both look into the eyes of their Master. Streams of ecstasy will penetrate through the eyes and permeate their hearts and souls. In this way, the disciples are blessed with the same divine virtues. As they have the same objective, the same ideal, the same ruling passion, they are naturally drawn to one another. A common grace flows through their frames, a common intoxication runs through their veins and binds them together in a common love for their Master. When two disciples are drawn to each other through the love of the Master, that love is always chaste and pious. They help each other without getting lost in sensuality, and move in harmony toward their ultimate goal.

People often ask how the relationship between a husband and wife can aid both partners in leading a spiritual life. The divine path, as taught by the Masters of Sant Mat, is not a path of negative mysticism where we leave our hearths and homes and live an ascetic life in the jungles. Ours is a path of positive mysticism in which we live regular family lives and discharge our worldly obligations. But we do so in a spirit of detachment. Marriage is no bar to spirituality. If you read the history of the saints you will find that many of them were family men who performed all their domestic duties. If a husband and a wife have a harmonious life and look in the same direction, which is towards the Master and God, they can help each other approach their goal in the least possible time. That does not mean they do not have love for each other. As God, or the Master, who is God-personified, is the source of all love, then both partners looking at that source are filled with the same love, and they will naturally have love for each other.

So in the realm of mysticism, two seemingly opposite definitions of love are correct. The first definition, which says that love consists in looking into each other's eyes, applies to the relationship between the Master and the disciple. But if the two disciples want to help each other on the spiritual path, then they do not look into each other's eyes. They follow the second definition of love and look in the same direction, toward the source of love. This fills them with mutual love, sympathy and compassion for each other, and enables them to move swiftly towards their goal.

CHAPTER EIGHTEEN
VEIL OF EGO

Until we gain complete control over our own selves and rise above the mind, intellect and ego, we cannot begin to make substantial progress on the path of spirituality. A Sufi poet has said that if there is anything which divides us from the Beloved it is the veil of ego. Our vanity is the greatest obstacle which stands in our path to God. If we examine our daily life we will find that our whole existence is based on the illusion of ego. We are always dwelling on our so-called superiority. But this feeling of self-exaltation is a delusion. The root cause of this ego lies in believing that we possess more intelligence, more wealth, and more power than anyone near us. A person enveloped in vanity becomes blind. Bereft of correct judgement, he cannot assess things in their true perspective. If we wish to travel Godwards, we must learn to overcome this obstacle, this veil of ego.

There are three aspects of the veil of ego: pride of knowledge, wealth and power. The first aspect of our ego is based on pride of intellect. Whether adult or child, each person thinks that his powers of reasoning and understanding are superior to others. Though we suffer from inherent limitations, paradoxically, each of us is convinced that he understands and judges best. This grand delusion charms and entices us into its net and it is only through the grace of God that we can escape it. We are elated to think that our power of understanding is not surpassed by anyone. It becomes easy under such a delusion to pursue one's course of action, thinking that one is in the right and can commit no wrong. Yet if we only stopped to think, it would be obvious that our understanding is strictly limited, that there are others with far greater knowledge and with far greater understanding. But in practice how many of us ever realize this? When we express our opinion, we think we are handing down the wisdom of Solomon, and our words seem nothing less than the revelations of the Lord Himself. We may think highly of our scientific advances, but our world of knowledge is ephemeral. The theory which is respected today is discarded tomorrow. When I was a child, Einstein's theory of relativity held the day. But since then there have been major changes and revisions. Such changes are not just confined to the realm of physics. They are there in every branch of knowledge. The whole field of medical science, for example, has undergone a revolution. When I was a boy if one had a fall and hurt oneself, hot fomentation was used to help cure the bad swelling. Today instead of hot fomentation we use an ice pack. Could the change in the treatment be more dramatic?

Even where intellectual knowledge extends itself to the study of religions it is still ephemeral. One scholar puts forward one interpretation and it seems as though that is the definitive interpretation. But soon another puts forward a different interpretation displacing the first, and so the process goes on. My own study of comparative religion has helped me to see the uncertainty of man's knowledge even when it extends to the domain of religion. Even at its best this knowledge is nothing but worldly knowledge, and what value has this knowledge as compared to the knowledge of the spirit? We take great pride in our mastery of science, of economics, of history, of anthropology, of literature, of this discipline or of that. And yet even if we have mastered all these fields of knowledge, what do they add up to? They give us knowledge only of the material world. Such knowledge does not constitute the truth. There is another knowledge, a knowledge which gives us access to the understanding of everything. The *Mundaka Upanishad* defines true knowledge as the knowledge which makes everything else known: i.e. knowledge of the higher self—the true man. If we know ourselves and know God, we understand everything. That knowledge, the knowledge of the spirit, is true wisdom. It is the basis of all other knowledge. While we have been pursuing material knowledge to its furthest limits we have alas been neglecting the spiritual knowledge. If our whole approach to knowledge is based on wrong premises, and we neglect the spiritual basis without which nothing stands, what is the use of all our efforts and attainments? If our very foundation is weak and faulty, how long and how strongly can it sustain a structure above it? The pride of intellect, of worldly knowledge, is a pride based on sand. No matter how extensive the domain of our worldly knowledge, it cannot take us to the truth. We think we are wise, but in reality we remain far from true wisdom. To reach the truth, we have to transcend worldly knowledge and rise into the spiritual realms of superconsciousness. This knowledge of the self and the Overself is, however, attained not through intellect but through surrender. It is the path of sacrifice, the path of love, the path of ecstasy, *janoon* (passion bordering on madness). In order to progress we have to surrender ourselves, forget ourselves, lose ourselves in complete identification with the object of our quest; then, and then alone, can we progress on the path of our spiritual evolution.

In the world of love, there is little room for ego, for vanity. The first thing we must renounce to proceed on the spiritual journey is our vanity. It is a strange path in which the apparent winner is in reality the loser. No one can boast of his success. This is the way of humility. This is the path on which we have to become "poor in spirit."

The second aspect of the veil of ego is that of wealth, of material possessions. How we pride ourselves on what we possess! We take pleasure in recalling all the businesses and factories we own. We delight in the acres that belong to us and the mansions which we call our own. And yet, how untrustworthy such possessions are! This was brought home so vividly to us at the time when India was partitioned. Those who owned vast farms, whole villages, were turned into refugees and prayed for their very lives. The wealth and the possessions on which they prided themselves, on which they anchored themselves, became the very cause of fear. Their lives were in danger because of the wealth that they had, and they prayed to the Lord to be saved, to be protected. They considered themselves lucky if they escaped with their lives, even if they left behind everything. The rich who had exploited the poor were suddenly reduced to poverty. The moneylenders had often lent money at such exorbitant rates that they could flourish on the interest alone. Now all their misbegotten wealth was reduced overnight to nothing, and they were compelled to taste the very poverty which they had mercilessly exploited. Those who had taken advantage of the poor, the helpless, the widows and the orphans, became themselves the object of the pity of others. The first blast of the storm, the first upheaval of the partition reduced them to nothing, and they were reduced to helplessness.

We were given a vivid demonstration of the nature of worldly possessions. A single turn of fate, a single event, and all that supported us was no longer there to support us. It has always been thus; indeed if we look around us, we find that vicissitudes and flux are inherent in the very nature of Dame Luck. Overnight, millionaires are reduced to bankruptcy. Those who are happy to be photographed and who are elated to see their pictures published in the papers, with one twist of fortune, slink away avoiding public gaze and ridicule.

What can our riches do for us in the hour of need? When Alexander, having conquered the world, fell ill, what could his gold and riches and possessions do for him? He begged his physician to let him live for an hour longer, for even half an hour—but his physician was helpless. As he told the world conqueror, "You speak of half an hour, but we cannot give you life for even half a breath, as life and death are not in our hands.'' As with the ego of intellect, the ego of possessions keeps us away from the Lord, and we must overcome it if we wish to tread the path of spirituality.

The third aspect of the veil of ego is the pride of power. We all delight in the authority we wield, and yet this ego is as weak and unsound in its foundation as the other aspects of ego. Even the mightiest of rulers are stripped of their power and authority in a moment. Those who control the destinies of millions are reduced to abject servitude overnight. We have witnessed recent events in different parts of the world. We do not even need to turn back to the pages of history. If we only stopped to think of what has happened within the past ten years, the lesson would be clear. We have seen a succession of individuals who sought to control the fate of a whole people, of an entire nation, of many nations put together, fall from the zenith of their power. Individuals who thought they were the masters of the lives of others were in no time stripped of their authority and reduced to a position of helplessness. And so we find that power and authority are of as little significance as worldly possessions and intellect.

All worldly knowledge, worldly possessions and worldly powers are ephemeral. They are illusory. Hiranya Kasipu, the famous Puranic king and father of Prahlad, declared, ''I am eternal, lord of the three worlds.'' He thought himself to be indestructible and believed that he would never die, and yet he was humbled and destroyed. Pharaohs of Egypt, when they were to die, had their courtiers and servants put to death so that they would not be without companions when they rose from death. They were audacious tyrants and committed terrible atrocities. Along with their courtiers and servants, they were embalmed after death, but never rose to life again, and have been reduced to dust. The only thing which does not perish is that which belongs to the spirit. Love, true love, is eternal and takes us beyond the limitations of time and space, and yet how few of us possess this gift? Do our kings and emperors possess it? Do our presidents, prime ministers and ministers possess it? Do our industrial lords and commercial magnates possess it? Do the chancellors of universities possess it? The fact is that the real knowledge, the real possession, the real power is that of the spirit which is the basis of divine and eternal virtues. It is the domain of those who have renounced everything, and who own nothing, of the prophets and sages who belong not even to themselves, and who are lost in the service of God. One of my verses is:

Although everything in this transitory
world is ephemeral,
I have brought here the eternal love
of the Lord with me.

The only real power is the power of the saints, but they wield it only for the good of others. The only real wealth is the wealth of Naam, the divine Word, and it is a wealth owned by the saints. The knowledge, the possessions and power which are eternal and changeless are alone real and these are the exclusive domain of the spirit. Our worldly knowledge, worldly possessions, and worldly power are always in flux and are ephemeral. What assurance or what anchorage can we find in them? Thus we find that the very basis of these three aspects of the veil of ego is false.

Our vanity is founded on that which cannot last and as such has no justification, no reality. If we could only understand and realize this, our whole process of reorientation would begin and we would turn our face to that which is spiritual, to that which is changeless. We need to develop right understanding so we can distinguish the eternal from the ephemeral. If we dispassionately analyze life and its problems, the right values of living will come home to us. Let us pray to God to enable us to have this right understanding so that we may tear down the veil of ego which divides us from the Beloved. This gift of transcending the ego, of becoming truly humble, is a divine gift. Let us pray, not only that our egoism be turned into humility, but that our vanity be turned into love. With the coming of these supreme virtues, we will be firmly on the path which leads us back to God. What is more, we will be well on the way to insuring peace and happiness in the world.

Is there any household where one finds its members living with each other in peace and harmony? Each home has been reduced to a battlefield. Whichever home you visit, wherever you go, there is tension of one ego clashing with another. Whether it is the children or the parents, the husband or the wife, the parents-in-law or the daughter-in-law, each is trying to get the better of the other. Each speaks as though his word were God's law. Each demands that his word be respected and not questioned. And when you make such demands, it is only because you believe that your powers of mind are unsurpassed by those of anyone else.

With the coming of humility and love, all this turmoil disappears. From a life of tension, competition and strife, we move to a life of harmony and peace. And when there is peace and harmony at home, there is a much better climate for meditation and for spiritual progress.

CHAPTER NINETEEN
VEGETARIAN DIET

The principles of spirituality have remained the same throughout the ages. Modern science is only now coming to the conclusions that the saints and mystics have realized and taught from time immemorial. In the realm of nutrition too, modern research is confirming the supremacy of the diet followed by those leading a spiritual life—the vegetarian diet. In all respects—spiritual, moral and physical—the vegetarian diet is the most suitable for man. And for those who wish to follow the path leading to self-knowledge and God-realization, a strict vegetarian diet is essential.

If we examine various religious and mystic traditions, we find that they recommend or require vegetarianism. Such a diet is associated with the earliest religious traditions. Pythagoras and those who followed his school of thought were vegetarians. Many of the famous early philosophers such as Plato, Empedocles, Apollonius, Plutarch and Porphyry also followed the vegetarian diet. Again, many of the early mystery religions, such as the Orphics and the Essenes had vegetarianism as a prerequisite for initiation. If we carefully study the holy Bible we find that God had originally intended man to be a vegetarian. In Genesis, God says: "I have given you every herb bearing seed which is upon the face of all the earth, and every tree, in which is the fruit of a tree yielding seed: To you it shall be for meat." And again: "I have given every green herb for meat." Even when God gave Moses the Ten Commandments, vegetarianism was necessarily implied. If we follow the commandment, "Thou shalt not kill," it is naturally out of the question to eat meat, fish, fowl or eggs. But the people, out of weakness, complained and said they could not keep the commandments, so Moses gave them more and more laws dealing with diet and other aspects of life. In the book of Isaiah in the Bible, God clearly says: "He who killeth an ox is as if he slew a man." After all, how can we claim to be lovers of God, lovers of His creation, if we kill the humbler members of God's family?

Jesus Christ was the Apostle of Peace; he was the embodiment of nonviolence. He taught, "Whosoever shall smite thee on thy right cheek, turn to him the other also." If he was nonviolent to that extent, could he have been violent to the lower rungs of God's creation—the animals, fowl and fish? Christ taught universal love and total nonviolence. He asked us not to indulge in any killing, and he commanded that we have love for all. If we were true followers of his teachings we could not kill and eat animals.

The Sufis of Persia were also vegetarians, and even today Sufis who practice zikr-e-ruhe, or simran of the soul, are vegetarians. Buddha, the Compassionate One, taught nonviolence toward all creatures, and originally his followers were vegetarians. Mahavira, the founder of the Jain religion preached a strict vegetarian diet. And of course, vegetarianism is an integral part of the Hindu religious tradition. Although most followers of the Sikh religion are not vegetarian now, at the Sikh temples no meat is served in the *langar* (free kitchen). And when the Sikhs observe a religious ceremony in their homes vegetarian meals are served after the recitation of the scriptures.

When the living Master or teacher leaves the earth, the esoteric side of his teachings is often lost or obscured in the rites and rituals which are created. Similarly, after the Master leaves, changes are made and relaxations in diet and discipline are allowed by those who want to popularize the religion or make it more acceptable to a larger number of people. But the mystic tradition is clear in advocating vegetarianism.

Many great philosophers, artists, poets and writers have been vegetarians as well. Albert Schweitzer, Leo Tolstoy, Percy Bysshe Shelley and Mahatma Gandhi are just a few examples. It was their sensitivity and compassion which led them to adopt the path of nonviolence toward all creation. There is an interesting anecdote from the life of George Bernard Shaw regarding the vegetarian diet. Once when he was very ill, the doctors said unless he started eating eggs and taking meat soup, he would die. As he was a strict vegetarian, he refused to follow the doctors' orders. When the doctors stuck to their point of view and told him they could not guarantee that he would survive the illness, G.B. Shaw called for his private secretary and in the presence of the doctors dictated his will. It said, "I solemnly declare that it is my last wish that when I am no longer a captive of this physical body, that my coffin when carried to the graveyard be accompanied by mourners of the following categories: first, birds; second, sheep, lambs, cows and other animals of the kind; third, live fish in an aquarium. Each of these mourners should carry a placard bearing the inscription: 'O Lord, be gracious to our benefactor G.B. Shaw who gave his life for saving ours!' "

Leonardo da Vinci, another vegetarian, had great compassion. Often when he passed by an open door and saw a caged bird, he would pay the owner for the cage and the bird. Then he would open the cage door and watch the joyful bird soar to freedom.

God has provided man with an abundance of fruits, vegetables, grains, legumes and herbs for food. And we can eat dairy products too, which do not require killing animals. The spiritual path is one of love, compassion and nonviolence. It is true that to live in this world, we must destroy some life; even the plants we eat and the bacteria we breathe have life. Every action has a reaction and the law of karma operates in the realm of diet, too. So the saints say that since we cannot do without food, we should choose the diet which causes the least possible pain, the least possible sin. In this regard, the ancient scriptures say that of the various life forms—man, animal, bird, reptile and plant—the least life force is in the plants. To explain this they say that there are five *tatwas* or creative and component elements which are earth, water, fire, air and ether. Man's body contains all five tatwas, and he is considered to be the highest and most valued in this creation. The killing of one's fellow man is regarded as the most heinous crime, and in history it has merited capital punishment. The next in value are the quadrupeds and beasts which have four tatwas or elements, with ether being absent, or forming a negligible portion. According to most laws, killing of an animal usually entails a penalty equal to the price of the animal in question. The third category includes birds, which have three active elements in them—water, fire and air. If someone kills a stray bird, he usually goes scot-free, and if a "protected" bird is killed the hunter may have to pay a small penalty for it. Lesser still is the value of reptiles, worms and insects which have only two active tatwas or elements—earth and fire, as the other three elements exist in a dormant form. The death of this species of life does not involve any penalty of payment according to most laws in this world. The least value is placed on roots, vegetables and fruits which contain only the element of water in an active state. Thus, karmically, the vegetarian or fruitarian diet is least pain-producing, and by adopting it, man contracts the least karmic debt. Since we have to keep our body going, then, keeping in view the goal of nonviolence, we should follow the vegetarian diet because it results in the least possible destruction.

Unfortunately, many people have misunderstandings about the nutritional value of the vegetarian diet, and they think it does not give us the proper food value. I have been in touch with leading nutritionists in India, and their evidence shows that a balanced vegetarian diet can certainly give us all the necessary nutrients. Until recently, the only real complaint about the vegetarian diet was that it did not provide the proper proteins. But the latest research confirms that the vegetarian diet definitely gives more than enough protein, as well as the required vitamins, minerals and calories. In fact, a number of doctors and nutritionists say that most people, including vegetarians, eat too much protein! As more and more research is conducted, scientists, biologists and nutritionists are finding that the vegetarian diet is the most wholesome and healthful.

The strongest animals with the greatest endurance are vegetarians. The elephant, the ox, and the horse are known for their might and capacity to work. We even measure the power of engines in "horsepower."

Even from the physiological point of view, man is most suited to a vegetarian diet—his physical structure does not place him in the same category as other meat-eating animals. For example, carnivorous animals have big cuspids, or canine teeth, as well as claws for ripping and tearing flesh; man does not. Man's teeth more closely resemble the vegetarian animals' which have special flat molars for grinding. Further, the intestines of meat-eating animals are short (about three times the length of the trunk of their body) so that the flesh is absorbed or expelled before it putrifies and produces poisons. But man and the vegetarian animals have very long intestines (about ten to twelve times the length of the trunk of their body). Again, the appetite of carnivorous animals is aroused by raw flesh and blood, but man is the only animal which eats meat that is cooked and camouflaged by spices and sauces.

If we stopped to think about it, we would realize that the food we eat has an effect upon our physical, emotional and mental makeup. If we are trying to lead a life of nonviolence and compassion, if we are trying to become more serene and peaceful, if we are trying to control our mind and senses, then we will naturally want to follow a diet that helps us achieve our goal.

Food can be categorized according to the effect it has upon man. In India, three broad categories of diet have been given: *satvik* or pure foods; *rajsic* or energizing foods; and *tamsic* or stupefying foods. Satvik foods include vegetables, grains, beans, legumes, fruits and nuts, as well as milk, butter and cheese in moderation. This diet produces serenity and equipoise, and it is said to keep the head and heart free from all types of impurities. Rajsic foods include pepper, spices, condiments and sour and bitter things. Foods of this type produce restlessness. Tamsic foods include stale foods, meat, fish, fowl, eggs and alcoholic beverages. A tamsic diet produces inertia. Taking these factors into view, the saints and sages from times immemorial followed the satvic diet because it is most helpful in leading a pure life conducive to spiritual advancement.

In terms of economics too, vegetarianism is the most practical diet. It takes ten acres of pastureland to produce a certain amount of meat protein, but the same amount of vegetable protein can be produced on only one acre of land. So nine acres of land are wasted when meat is produced. Similarly, an animal eats sixteen pounds of grain to produce only one pound of meat, and thus fifteen pounds of grain are wasted. God has given us the facilities and bounties of nature by which all His children can be fed. But if we look around we see that millions of people all over the world are dying of starvation. We should have compassion for our fellow man; our hearts should be moved by the suffering of others. At the very least we should make the best use of what God has given us. Vegetarianism is much more productive and much less wasteful. So in this regard too, the vegetarian diet is the most humane, rational and compassionate.

In addition to being careful about what type of food we eat, we should also be careful about how much we eat. The basic principle with regard to food is, "Eat to live, not live to eat." Unfortunately most of us live to eat—and overeat. When we are given a new or delicious dish, we overeat. When we gather with our friends and relations, we overeat. And sometimes to show someone we appreciate their hospitality, we overeat. But overeating is the cause of many of our health problems, and some of our meditation problems as well. The Persian mystic Sheikh Saadi has said that because we are filled up to our noses with food, we are not able to see the Light of God. He advised that the stomach be divided into four compartments: two for filling with simple food; one for water; while reserving one for the Light of God.

If we eat too much we feel sleepy and drowsy, and for those on the spiritual path, more time spent sleeping means less time for meditation. And even when we do meditate, if we overeat we may be drowsy. Once a man went to a saint and complained, "Sir, my meditations are not good." The saint replied, "Look to your stomach." Another man came to this saint and said, "I can't control my mind." The saint replied, "Look to your stomach." A third man came and said, "I am not having good health." And the saint again replied, "Look to your stomach." So eating less than we have an appetite for is good not only for our meditations but also for our health.

Diet is indeed an important aspect of the spiritual life. If we wish to follow the path of nonviolence and love for all creation, then we will adhere to a strict vegetarian diet. In doing so, we will not only have compassion on the younger members of God's creation, and our fellow man, but we will also have compassion on our own selves.

CHAPTER TWENTY
AIR-CONDITIONING

Earlier today the air-conditioning in this hotel was not working properly and we were all feeling rather restless and somewhat uncomfortable. Why? because we have moved far away from nature. We are addicted to artificial material comforts. We cannot live without air-conditioning, and we use it from dawn to dusk and dusk to dawn. In our homes, we cannot live without refrigerators, and gadgets in which utensils and clothes are cleaned by the push of a button.

God made man and blessed him with the necessary gifts of nature. When man's life was simple, when his needs were few, when he could adapt himself to natural circumstances, he was happier. He did not need air-conditioning; he did not need refrigerators and sophisticated gadgets. We ourselves are making our lives more prone to difficulties, for when we have to go without these artificial comforts we are unhappy. Even in India people are getting used to such conveniences, and because India has almost daily power crises they must also get used to the failure of the equipment which produces these comforts. The result of these power failures is that people become restless. When I ask them, "What about your meditations?" they say, "Our air-conditioner or fan didn't work, so we couldn't sit for meditation." Yet they do not find any difficulty in spending time to prepare themselves to greet each other at work or at restaurants and theaters.

These man-made conveniences have become like a drug addiction. Once a person is addicted to them he cannot function without them, he cannot live without them.

It is our dependence on such artificial comforts and conveniences which has made us used to solo playing in life, rather than playing as a part of the orchestra. The Masters have always stressed community life, they have stressed that we should have love and compassion for the entire community of God. But our dependence on modern facilities has caused each of us to lead a life of aloofness, a life of individuality. We are content to lead our independent lives without any interference and without any connection with others. And this is what is called "enjoying the fruit of progress, and leading independent lives." Progress and independence are fine, and we should try to make the best of advances in technology and science, but all the same, we should not cut ourselves off from our fellow man. If we do so, we defeat the purpose for which we have been created: to have love and compassion, and to share the weal and woe of all mankind, and of the entire creation. But unfortunately our independence has reached such an extent that no one seems to know or care about his fellow beings. And thus, the virtues of community life, of fellow-feeling, of love and compassion for all, are naturally lost sight of. If we do not come in contact with others, how can we have love for them?

We have forgotten all about living as members of the human community, and as a result I find that we do not even know about the welfare of our own neighbors. This situation is so extreme that when I talk to those from the West, I am surprised to hear that they do not even know about the welfare of their own relatives! There is such a breakdown in family life that parents do not know much about their children, and children do not know much about their parents. I find that some mothers and fathers have not seen their children for decades! Similarly, many people do not even know where their own brothers and sisters are living. It is so surprising, but it seems to have become the way of life now!

We say that we believe in the biblical commandment, "Love thy neighbor as thyself," but how many of us really practice this principle? On how many occasions are we aware that our neighbor is in need of something, is writhing in pain or even dying of starvation? How often have we visited our neighbors, particularly those who happen to be poor, maimed, helpless, aged, physically deformed or unable to earn their own livelihood? How many times a week, a month, even a year have those of us who are healthy, financially secure, and respected in the community, visited such neighbors in need? During one week we go to so many places of enjoyment: to a night club for dancing, to a music festival, to a museum, to an art gallery. And we spend so much time entertaining our friends. We go on dates to the movies, eat out at restaurants and go on picnics. Each week we have one hundred sixty-eight hours at our disposal. How much time do we spend on going out to places of enjoyment, and how much time do we spend on visiting our neighbors in need? How many of us spend even one hour helping others? Most of us do not even know if we have suchlike neighbors. Each of us leads an individualistic life. We remain isolated in our air-conditioned homes cut off from mankind. And even in our homes we remain in our air-conditioned rooms, oblivious of our own relatives. How can we know about the suffering of others unless we lead a community life? Our addiction to pleasure and artificial comforts has become so great that, like the Lotus-eaters, we have become oblivious to everyone around us. We should not be so ease-loving that we fail to be concerned with our fellow man. It is time that we hark back to nature and emerge from the isolation of our artificial lives of self-interest and independence. If we feel restless when our air-conditioners do not work, then we should feel more restless when we are out of tune with the hearts of our fellow beings.

Instead of being content with solo playing, we should become part of the orchestra, and play in harmony with others. The musicians in an orchestra must be constantly aware that they are members of a larger unit and they must also be aware of the roles of all the other members. Similarly, we should play our roles in the orchestra of life so that we create a symphony of love and peace which reverberates throughout the universe.

CHAPTER TWENTY-ONE
PARENTS
AND
CHILDREN

The budding hopes for the future of man
Lie in the children of today.

Children should be allowed to preserve and develop the gifts of purity, of simplicity, of wonder, of concentration and love with which they are born. We adults lose these blessings as we grow older, and it is imperative that we seek to revive and develop them if we wish to become conscious of the beauty and grandeur of God's creation and thereby become His beloved children.

If we wish to escape the sufferings of this world, if we wish to gain eternal peace and ecstasy, if we wish to attain the supreme goal of life and become one with our Creator, then in character and action we must become as little children. All saints have laid great emphasis on childhood. Even among today's prominent thinkers the call comes, "Catch them while they are young!" To accomplish anything substantial in life the foundation is best laid in childhood. If one is to become a great leader the molding of one's temperament, one's character and life-style must begin in these early years. No matter what field of knowledge or what skill you choose, if you wish to attain proficiency, excellence and perfection, then the molding, training, and appropriate impressions must begin quite early. William Wordsworth has said, "The child is the father of the man," and we see how the lives of great people are foreshadowed by rays of greatness in childhood.

The simplicity, purity, and sense of wonder within children, and their amazing capacity to respond to love, endears them to the hearts of all. They are embodiments of love and are saturated with it. Whoever reaches out to them becomes theirs. We who have seen our childhood and youth fade fast from our memory need to gaze again at our children in whom an ever-fresh source of inspiration, wonder and divinity is waiting to be tapped.

Children are closer to the Creator, and to His creation. Children are like small pools in which we can receive clear, cool and refreshing reflections of God's qualities. In children we can get a glimpse of His image, the image from which man was fashioned. They who have just come from the divine regions above, reveal His radiance on their faces. Children are signposts which remind us of our heavenly abode. We have a great deal to learn from them that we ourselves have forgotten, a great deal that we have lost. We too entered life with their gifts but as time moved on step by step, we became lost in selfishness, and the divine qualities which we had brought with us disappeared slowly from our sight. The further we moved away from our early years, the further we moved away from our true nature, and from God.

If we wish our children to grow up into model individuals, we must first become model parents. The impressions we create have a far-reaching influence on our children. Hazur Baba Sawan Singh used to say that a child is like a blank sheet of paper. Just as you can write what you please on a blank piece of paper, you can engrave whatever impressions you like on the mind of a young child. If the impressions are positive, our children will grow in strength with the years. First they will grow into ideal citizens of their state. Then they will develop into ideal citizens of their nation, ideal citizens of the world, and ultimately ideal citizens of the cosmos.

It is essential that we recognize the importance of the earliest phases of life. The first impressions the child receives form the foundations on which he stands ready to step into the world. These early impressions are thus the most important, and they are formed by the parents—and especially the mother. The mother plays an extremely important part in the upbringing of the child. The first stage of a child's education occurs in the womb of the mother. Her thoughts have a great effect on the child. From the moment of conception, through the period the child is in the mother's womb, the thoughts and radiation of the mother lay the foundation for the child's development. Spiritually evolved souls have emphasized the necessity of chastity from the day conception takes place until the child is weaned from the mother's breast. This period of chastity coupled with prayer and meditation has a benevolent and elevating effect on the child. Before and after birth, the mother can bestow upon the child the greatest boon by surrounding him in an atmosphere spiritually surcharged by selfless love. If the mother spends her time in remembrance of God and is herself attuned to the Music of the Spheres and the Light of God, she radiates those spiritual bounties, those heavenly gifts to the child, and a firm foundation will be set for the child to grow up to be a spiritually evolved soul.

Historically in India, mothers have been spiritually minded and have played an important role in the children's development. The saints and seers of old have often compared the love of a perfect Master for his disciples to that of a mother for her children. The highest form of love comes from a perfect Master, because he expects nothing in return from his disciples; his way of life is to give, give and give. The nearest comparison to the Master's love is that of the mother for the child because the mother serves the child so selflessly. The mother sacrifices everything for the child; at times she even goes without meals for the sake of feeding her baby. In the East small children sleep with their mother, and on the coldest nights in December and January, when the child makes water on one side of the bed the mother moves to that wet and cold side of the bed herself and puts the child on the warm side. A mother has to do so much for the upbringing and nourishment of the child, giving up all thought of her own self. But these days what is generally happening, is that the ties between the mother and the child are becoming more and more tenuous. Not long ago the practice of breastfeeding almost disappeared. And the concept of leading a life of chastity during the period of pregnancy has almost vanished. In our so-called advanced and modern age the child is brought up more by baby-sitters and nurses than by the mother, and the bond between the child and the mother is weakening every day.

The parents are the vine and the children are the branches. The children should normally be embedded in their parents, and the parents should engraft themselves in their children. Parents who strive to be ideal will be prepared to sacrifice their social engagements and their club life to devote their time first to the creation of images of greatness in themselves, and then to the transmission of these images to their children.

I often hear the complaint these days that the youth are undisciplined, that they do not respect and honor us, that they cannot apply themselves to their studies or work, and that they cannot do anything with unwavering concentration. If we study the problem dispassionately, do we not find that we are ultimately responsible for our children's failings? A child is a very keen observer and no action of ours escapes his notice. What is it that the child observes about us? Does he not observe our callousness towards the needs of our fellow brethren, and our gross vanity? Does he not feel in his heart of hearts our lack of reverence for God, and our disregard for prayer and meditation? When our elders come to visit he watches us greet them with love and respect, but he sees that when they turn their backs we treat them as objects of ridicule. Again, he notices that we pay so many compliments to our friends and neighbors, but as soon as they have stepped beyond our threshold we begin criticizing them. We think that the child is not observing us, that he is too young to notice the disparity between our actions in public and private. The fact is that there is no keener observer than the child. It is not our children that we are fooling, it is only ourselves. The child sees that our lives have no integrity, no honesty, no truthfulness. Cut loose from our anchorage in the positive virtues, our lives are devoid of faith and conviction in the limitless potential of man— man who resides in the ever-present shadow of the greatness of God. We are without poise or balance because we lack a steady center in life. Children, with their purity of vision, see our lives are filled with hypocrisy and deception.

Children are fascinated by and often play with masks, which in my childhood could be purchased for a few pennies each. Animal masks such as tigers, monkeys, dogs and wolves were very popular and we went on changing them as we played. Whereas we would wear dozens of masks as children, as adults we wear innumerable masks; we have a mask to suit each new situation. As I expressed it once in a verse, "On the countenance of each friend I behold every mask and every color." The child sees us caught up in this game of masks, and notes how we change from one mask to the other: now playing the tiger, now the lamb; now appearing the image of friendliness, now the very opposite. Seeing this chameleon-like quality in us, seeing our proneness to hypocrisy, how can he hold us in respect? How can he revere us? When a child sees that his parents speak about selfless service but turn their backs on the poor and downtrodden, he loses all respect for them. When he finds that his parents project one image to the world but practice just the reverse of it at home, he is more than convinced that what his parents say is only an outward show without any reality. Such a child loses all respect for his parents, and this is how we begin putting the nails in our own coffins. It is at this stage that the child revolts, and loses his mainstay in life. He learns not to trust anybody; he learns not to respect anybody; he learns not to anchor himself in anything. In short, he loses faith in life and becomes incapable of self-discipline or concentration. The lack of self-discipline and the lack of respect for elders that we observe among the young are failings for which we ourselves are directly responsible.

If the parents lead an ideal life, if they are humble, if they are truthful, if they have the qualities of self-sacrifice, of selfless service, of chastity and of non-violence, then these qualities become imbedded in their children. I vividly remember the ideal example set by my revered father, Sant Kirpal Singh. When I was a schoolboy I often worked late into the night, but whenever I went to bed I saw my beloved father still busy at his writing. In those days he was working on the *Gurmat Sidhant*, a monumental book on all aspects of spirituality. When I awoke I always found my father sitting in meditation. I also had to spend time in meditation. It was inescapable, for no breakfast would be served unless we sat for our meditation. I always found him busy, he was never idle. Life at home was centered on truth; a word once given was kept. We never saw our parents criticizing others. There were many who came to see my father and if any of them began criticizing somebody else, my father would change the subject saying, "Why not discuss something involving our own good instead of criticizing others?"

We used to witness a continuous stream of visitors coming to see my father. They had all kinds of problems and he always listened to them with the utmost sympathy. If someone was in financial difficulty, he would help that person monetarily. If someone was greatly distressed and disturbed, he would bring him to my room and have him sit in meditation. If somebody had a problem, he would make a note of it in his diary and see if he could remedy the situation by speaking to someone who would be helpful. If he found anyone in extreme anguish, he would even offer to go to his own Master, Hazur Baba Sawan Singh, and speak of it to him. During the day my father was busy at the office. When he came home from work, he would have a simple meal and then set off to visit the sick and needy in the hospitals or in their homes. His life was totally dedicated to the service of God's creation and the consummation of his soul's journey in union with his Master and God. Thus, service and devotion were two poles on which his life turned. His whole existence was embedded in humility, and an inexpressible sweetness radiated an inner peace to all who came in contact with him. What a great heart he had. He listened to each person with so much patience, and so much sympathy.

How could such surroundings not have an appropriate influence on the mind of a child? How different, how unlike this is the upbringing we give to our young.

The positive development of the child at home should be supplemented by the education process at school. Ideally, teachers should work selflessly for the education of their students, engrafting their good qualities and knowledge into them. Unfortunately, the child now finds that like his parents, his teachers also profess one thing but act in the reverse manner. Because of this, the child loses faith in humanity. The result is he neither believes in human values nor in social values, let alone the question of spiritual and cosmic values. If this happens, then he enters society like a rudderless ship swayed to and fro on the stormy sea of life. This is the bane of our present civilization. In our time there was engrafting between the teacher and the taught. Our teachers and professors treated us with great love and we also looked up to them with great respect. They often called on us at home and instructed us on subtle points which needed extra clarification. At college our professors vied with one another to help us. If one of their students topped the university in his grade average, it provided the teacher with a source of delight and great satisfaction. The involvement that our teachers and professors had in the instruction of their students was as intense and sincere as that of a parent. I am afraid that this process of engrafting is seldom seen in our modern world. Now, students have little or no respect for teachers. And when students lack respect for their teachers, how will their teachers be inspired to slave for them? When teachers are not given the respect they deserve, when they are underpaid and not given their rightful place of honor, then naturally they lose heart, too. The lack of discipline which parents complain of at home has spread to schools, colleges, and universities. It is fast becoming the seed of social disintegration.

If true engrafting is to take place successfully, it is

imperative that the plant which receives the graft be capable of accepting it. You cannot graft a mango on a thistle. In human terms this capacity to receive is known as receptivity. A student is able to direct his attention to his teacher or Guru and assimilate what he says only if his early childhood training has equipped him for it. That is why all spiritual seers lay so much emphasis on the impressionable years. It is in this phase that the appropriate kind of receptivity can be created. This is the reason children born in a charged aura of spirituality are especially blessed. They receive the right kind of uplifting and ennobling influence and become more receptive students and disciples. If the home atmosphere is good and it is both complemented and supplemented by the education in school, then the impact of the two on the child is so great and so indelible that no unhealthy outside influence can ever erase it.

While the knowledge our parents and teachers have to give is worldly, the knowledge given by a true Guru or Master is an esoteric one; by receiving this knowledge, everything else becomes known. It is through the process of receptivity to a true spiritual Master, to one who is himself imbedded in God, that the goal of life can be fulfilled. This process of learning is the true engrafting. The plant which receives the graft retains its essential quality and character, yet it acquires all the characteristics of the one which is grafted to it. When a Guru or teacher engrafts himself to a student, he does not crush the student's originality. He encourages the student's originality, and he polishes it. And the end product is the best combination of both student and teacher. This is what a Guru endeavors to do. Our earthly teachers concern themselves with one limited area or another, but the Master seeks to transform the entire person.

Receptivity is at its height in early childhood. The receptive nature of children should be an example and lesson to us. The Granth Sahib, the holy scripture of the Sikhs, exhorts us to go to the Guru like a child. A child is not hampered by preconceptions. He does not bring rigid notions to bear on what he experiences. If he receives love from anyone he is willing to respond without question of social, religious or political relationships. His world knows nothing of mine and thine. On the other hand, we as adults are restricted by our preconceptions. We are always testing and checking. When we hear a saint speak we keep telling ourselves, "Oh, this is what is said in the Vedas, this is what is said in the Bible, this has been said in the Koran or in the Granth Sahib." If we could be like a child when we come to the feet of a Master we could be drinking in every word, we would be all eyes, taking in every lyrical glance. It is precisely this capacity for total receptivity which is characteristic of childhood, and this is what we need to cultivate on the spiritual path. If we approach a saint with such total childlike receptivity, then we will begin to absorb whatever he has to give. Then the principle and process of grafting will take place and we will be steadily transformed. Just as water flows from a higher to a lower level, if we have a childlike receptivity the godly qualities and virtues of the spiritual Master will flow into us and the process of grafting will be fulfilled.

It is time we begin to play our part. If we as disciples

do not live our lives by the teachings given by the saints, then we are false to them, and false to ourselves. We will subsequently fail in our most sacred trust of properly raising the children with whom God has blessed us. It is bad enough if we fail to reform our lives for the sake of our own selves. It is infinitely worse if we fail to do so as parents, for then we are adversely affecting not only our own lives, but the lives of our children whom God has entrusted to our care. Let us begin now to fashion a way of life which is marked by love, sweetness, humility, discipline and selfless service. Let us help create a setting in which there is respect for truth, and respect for the parents, the teachers and the Gurus. If we create such a pattern it will surely have its impact on the young. If we can provide our children with the right start in life they will move from strength to strength as years go by.

It is said a high point comes in our life when we cease to live for ourselves and begin to live for our children. Goals which we never attempted to achieve for ourselves are suddenly reached when we have the resolve and the strength to attempt them for our children. We need to adopt this way of thinking if we wish our children to grow up into noble and worthy citizens. And to do this, we also need to learn from them. The child is not subject to deception, hatred or selfishness. For progress on the spiritual path we have to develop in ourselves their freedom from preconceptions and from prejudices. We have to develop their capacity for love. We have to cultivate their tenderness, simplicity, and receptivity. If we can sit like a child at the feet of a Master, we will absorb his teachings and will be well on our way to reaching our spiritual goal—communion of our soul with God. The world may consider us foolish, but the results will show us as the wisest of the wise. Living by the precepts of the saints, we will turn our own lives into model ones, and we will not only radiate peace and discipline at home, but we will also move steadily towards the ultimate goal of life which beckons us to the highest spiritual realms.

PART III

ALCHEMY
OF
LOVE

CHAPTER TWENTY-TWO
WAITING
FOR THE
BELOVED

If we are really waiting for our Beloved to arrive, for the Master of our heart to arrive, for somebody who has snatched our heart away, for somebody who has caused us poignancy and grief, yearning and pining, longing and torture, then waiting has its own charm, waiting has its own bliss. Sometimes we wait for our Beloved. A few minutes pass. The Beloved does not appear. A few more moments pass. The Beloved has not yet arrived, but with the passage of time our intensity, our craving, our desire for him becomes greater and greater. A few more moments pass. Our eyes are fixed on the door. The Beloved still eludes us, and that causes our heart to melt and gush out of our eyes. But the Beloved has not yet come. There is some sound produced by the footsteps of a stranger; our heart starts to beat more violently, but to our dismay and despair, disillusionment and disappointment, the Beloved has not yet come. The wind begins to blow, and the leaves of the trees start to rustle. Once again we think that it is our Beloved's footsteps, but still our eyes, our whole being now converted into one eye, does not see the cynosure of our heart. Ultimately, a stage comes when it appears that the very beat of our heart is the sound of the footsteps of the Beloved.

Just look at the cruelty of Nature. It is mocking us, it is playing pranks with us, so much so that the rustle of the leaves of a tree, the footsteps of a man unknown to us, and ultimately our own heartbeat play tricks and pranks on us. During this time of waiting, it is my own experience—and it must be the experience of many of you—that while we have been thinking of the one Beloved, the one Master of our soul, the one Lord of our heart, the one object of our vision, we have become quite oblivious of ourselves. We have even forgotten the environment in which we are sitting. We are oblivious of those sitting next to us. We have only one thought, one object, one longing, one desire, and that is to see the effulgent, resplendent, glorious countenance of the Beloved. In this agony of anticipation, we are one with him. Our whole body has now become one eye which is constantly and wistfully looking towards the door. Our whole being is one big ear which is trying to listen for the footsteps of our Beloved. But the Beloved comes not. So you see, if our longing is real and intense, then we actually become one with the Master. We feel the presence of the Master, and it is not that we only *feel* the presence of the Master, we may also *experience* the physical presence of the Master. A true Master can manifest himself even physically at thousands of places at the same time.

I can tell you from my own experience that I have undergone this torture of waiting which I have de-

scribed. I have even tried to express this torture in one
of my verses:

Is it in reality the sound of someone's
*   footsteps?*
Is it in reality the enrapturing tune of
*   the Celestial Musician?*
Or is it the beat of my heart which is
*   playing tricks on me?*

I have sometimes passed such moments of self-
obliviousness, moments which have changed into moments of bliss, into moments of ecstasy because I find
my Master face to face with me. I have paid obeisance
to his lotus feet, he has taken me in his arms, he has
patted me, and then, since he is the gracious Master, the
most gracious Master that the world has ever seen, he
has not only taken me in his arms, but he has talked to
me within. And then he has taken me above body-
consciousness, taken me with him to the higher planes,
leaving the stars, the moon and the sun behind, making
me one with him in his radiant form, in his effulgent
form. He has taken me into moments of eternity,
beyond the limitations of time and space, and then giving me a glance of love and a boost on the higher planes,
he has taken me into the highest realms of spirituality.
On the way he has introduced me to the various Masters
who have blessed this earth since time immemorial, and
arranged for our conversation. We have conversed in a
language which has no tongue, which has no words, and
which has no alphabet. We have conversed in a
language which is eternal, which divine lovers even now
speak. It is the language which will continue to the end
of all time. That has been the Master's grace.

After taking me to our Eternal Home, Sach Khand, he has taken me on to higher realms known as Agam and Agochar, those regions which are fathomless, those regions which are beyond human imagination. And after that we reached Anami, the ultimate region which has no shores, which has no limitations, which has no name. We can name all things when we are on the physical plane, when we are on the astral plane, when we are on the causal plane—but when we go beyond these planes, words fail us and all that we can cry out is that we are of the same essence as of God. As we progress spiritually our passion and zeal become more and more intensified to reach the lotus feet of our munificent Creator. And all this is attained through a process which is the most perfect science.

Whereas spirituality on the one hand can be called the most perfect science, paradoxically enough, on the other hand, it can be called the most perfect art. It is the art of igniting the divine fire which is dormant within and which can raise us on the wings of the Celestial Music and the Light of God.

Thus, waiting is a blessing. I quite believe that it has its own anguish, its own pain, its own yearning and pining. And at times it appears that its intensity is going to drain all life out of us, yet that same waiting can be transformed into bliss and tranquility and result in the ultimate communion of the soul with the Creator. The vigil of waiting for the Beloved leads to the first stage of communion with the Almighty. It is the first step on the path to our Eternal Home. It is the first move in the journey through an endless ocean of tears which ultimately takes us to the fountainhead of all ecstasy, of all joy, of all bliss, and helps us in losing our identity and attaining our ultimate communion with the Lord of Lords, with the Master of Masters, with the Supreme Creator. One poet has said:

> *Fulfillment is reached when the fire*
> *of love burns in lover and Beloved*
> *with the same intensity.*

So it was not just all of you waiting for me; I was also waiting for you, probably with a greater intensity. But this is a path on which we have to observe a certain mode of conduct, a certain mode of life which has been described in various ways by various lovers from time immemorial.

Another poet has said:

> *There are customs and there are practices*
> *Which should be observed by those who*
> *imbibe from the overflowing bounty of*
> *the divine Cupbearer.*

There is a code of conduct whose rigors we all have to pass through before we become good tipplers; we have to inculcate self-discipline which is imperative on any path. Generally it is thought that when tipplers drink, they are out of their senses, and they say whatever they like in a fit of intoxication, and behave in a manner which is not approved of by society. But for a tippler of the divine wine there is always a code of conduct to be observed, and those tipplers have always adhered to its observance. That code has its own rigors, its own hazards, its own eccentricities and idiosyncrasies. So the path of the Masters is the path of love. And on this path we have to undergo many ordeals, and those ordeals—which may be insurmountable ordeals from the point of view of worldly people—are the way of life for those who learn to follow this path.

Again, we are told that the spiritual path is a path of patience and perseverance. It is a path of constant waiting for the Beloved, and therefore we have to get used to the eccentricities and idiosyncrasies of the Beloved. Waiting has its own charm and has been described in the literature of the mystics as an important subject which has not only to be understood but to be practiced by those who traverse this path. It is a path of tears, it is a path of pining, it is a path of longing, it is a path of waiting. In our modern age we expect everything to keep to a schedule; ours has become a push-button society, so we feel spirituality should also work in accordance with the rules of the push-button era. Whenever we want to have the Beloved with us we want him to come according to a proper schedule. Suppose somebody is initiated today; he expects that after two months he should be able to rise above body-consciousness, and after a few more months he expects to merge with his Master, and shortly thereafter to attain communion with the Almighty. But it is not so easy, and progress is not so mechanical on the path of spirituality. On this path we have to adjust ourselves to the Beloved's rules of conduct, which to our mind may seem eccentric. But they are strictly in conformity with the rules which govern the path and which govern the conduct of those who are on the path. And three important aspects of the path are patience, perseverance and waiting for the Beloved.

In romantic literature it appears that the beloved

always eludes the lover, yet the lover continues to wait. It is the same in the spiritual realm. One of my verses says:

> *The meeting with the Beloved is*
> *nothing but a continuous promise.*
> *When one night passes you must wait*
> *for the next.*

This is a path in which we have to wait for the Beloved for night after night, and although the Beloved may give us many promises, those promises only mature at the proper time. They are fulfilled at a preordained time, and howsoever restless we may feel, we have to undergo the lover's code of conduct and wait patiently, long patiently, pine patiently for the Beloved to come. But as I have said, waiting has its own charm.

Waiting for the Beloved has various stages. As I have already described, the first stage is when we look at our watch; the appointed time has arrived—the time on the schedule—but the Beloved has not come. We get a little restless, but then, knowing the code of conduct on the path of love, we go on waiting. We know this is not a path in which we fix an appointment at seven-thirty in the evening and if the Beloved does not appear we close our door and go away. It is a path in which if we are really in love with the Beloved we wait for the Beloved. Seven-thirty comes, the Beloved is not there, so we continue waiting. Then slowly our heartbeat starts increasing. We look for the Beloved with all longing, with all pining, with all restlessness. At first, we look towards the door time and again to see if our Beloved has come. Sometimes we walk to the main entrance to see if the Beloved has arrived. But the Beloved has not come. So we continue waiting, still longing for the Beloved, and still pining for the Beloved. Then there is a flutter in the air, and the flutter causes a rustling of the leaves in a tree, and the moment we listen to the rustling of the leaves we think that probably it is the sound of the footsteps of the Beloved. With every sound we rush out of the room to see whether the Beloved is coming. But we find that we still have to go on waiting patiently. Time passes and still the Beloved has not yet come. We are obliged to go on waiting and waiting until in the end, we find that the very beat of our heart appears to be the sound of the footsteps of the Beloved. That is the moment when we are entirely in tune with the Beloved, when we are entirely one with the Beloved. And it is at that stage, when we are burning for the Beloved, that the Beloved finally appears.

So waiting is a rule rather than an exception on the path of love. It is one of this path's unique features, and those who wish to traverse this path have to observe its code of conduct. We have to give time to our meditations. We have to build up a base with an ethical life, then we have to wait patiently for a boost, and that boost comes through the lyrical glances of the Beloved. But for us to be lucky enough to get those glances we have to wait, we have to pine, we have to yearn for them with all intensity. And then when those glances come, we are able to traverse the path successfully.

Many of my brothers and sisters, sons and daughters, come to me and say, "We have been initiated for the last two months, we have been initiated for the last six months, and still we have not made sufficient progress within." And when I ask them how much time they have put in meditation, they tell me that they are meditating for half an hour, and that on some days they miss it entirely. I always tell them, "When you want to meet your beloved in this world, you are willing to wait for hours on end. If this is true of your worldly beloved, then how much more perseverance will be needed to have union with the Eternal Beloved?"

When we find that the love of our Beloved is engrained in our very being, that our entire being is permeated with the love of the Beloved, that if our veins are cut we will not find blood but only the love of the Beloved flowing there, then at that stage, the form of the Beloved appears in our meditation. I am told by doctors, that so far as antibiotics are concerned, they do not start functioning unless they have achieved a certain level of concentration in the blood. When we take the first tablets or injections, they do not start functioning all of a sudden. We have to absorb a certain amount of these antibiotics before they start working. So on the spiritual path also, we have to wait patiently until we have arrived at a certain level, and once we have arrived there then the spiritual blessings become effective of their own accord, and we automatically receive the blessings of the Master within. At this stage we will be blessed with the glimpses of the Master within, and not only within, but sometimes outwardly also. Let us go on waiting for the Beloved, yearning for the Beloved, and let us do so with a firm conviction that we will attain union. Union is a must. But that union comes at the appointed hour. That union comes when we are saturated with the thought of the Beloved at all times.

CHAPTER TWENTY-THREE
PANGS
OF
LOVE

One who has never tasted the fruits of spirituality cannot know what that taste is like. Spirituality is not a business; it is a path of faith and constant self-surrender. The very basis of spirituality is love. It is a continuous struggle, a continuous restlessness of the heart. As soon as a person tastes just a little of this divine love, he craves for more—such is its sweetness. Naturally, one cannot get enough of this love; so however much we may have, we always want more. We can never be satisfied until we reach our Eternal Home, and thereafter have complete communion with our Beloved. Having come from that Eternal Home we cannot know of lasting peace and joy until we are re-united with Him from whom we came. Once united, our bliss is complete and it knows no end. It is an ocean which has no shores, no limits.

Love is so vast that the moment we taste it we can only crave for more and more. However much we taste, however large our share, we are never satisfied. That is why the saints have said that this is not a path of dryness. We have only to think of our Beloved, and tears of longing start to flow from our eyes. The mystics have described this as one of the signs of a true lover of God. When we are fortunate enough to meet the Master, to taste a little of his divine love, to become saturated with that love, then tears of love, repentance, and confession begin to flow; we become aware of how we have wasted our lives. Rabi'a Basri, the great eighth century mystic, was once asked if God came to her first and then she started her prayers, or if she started her prayers and then God came to her. She replied, "I can only say this: When tears start rolling down from my eyes in sweet remembrance of the Lord, then the clouds have come and the rain will follow." Our tears pave the way for our ultimate communion with the Lord, and we can never be satisfied until we are fully drenched in His love.

This love is the golden key that opens the door to the Kingdom of Heaven. Without love nothing has ever been achieved, nor can be achieved on this Path. But it is difficult to understand the meaning of love, its purpose and scope. It is only through the Master that we can understand love, and it is he who allows us to develop it. Love is as boundless as God Himself. To know its full meaning is beyond our limited comprehension. It is only faith and surrender to the Beloved that can allow us to know something of it, to taste its sweetness. The tenth Sikh Guru, Guru Gobind Singh, said, "Verily, verily, I say unto you, they alone who love have found God." We should try to abide by this advice, for there is no other way.

Because the Master is an embodiment of love, it is he

who comes to save us. He solves our problems in ways we cannot fully understand. And then, it is his sustaining power of love that helps us through our mundane lives from day to day. Swami Ji Maharaj says that the Naam Power is looking after us every moment. And a Persian poet has said, "My Father knows my needs more than I do, and is continuously watching over me; if I were to be left to look after my own problems, there would be nothing but headaches for me." So that Power is not only looking after the whole universe, but it is sustaining each one of us. Unless we come in contact with and taste that Power of love, we become caught up in the hold of the world.

The mystics say that behind every moment of joy, there is concealed pain. One of my verses says:

Every joy which came my way, had hidden
deep within it a great anguish;
Not one moment of my life has passed
without pain.

Even when we enjoy some moments of happiness and bliss, these are transitory; our sorrow and pain are more lasting. This path of spirituality is a continuous process of pining and yearning for the Beloved. How can we be satisfied without Him? Look at the life of the Beloved Master, Sant Kirpal Singh. It was a continuous endeavor, a continuous struggle. As a child he longed to spend his life in selfless service. Then he had an intense desire to go to the feet of a perfect Master and that quest was marked by much anguish and pain. Finally, when he came to Hazur Baba Sawan Singh, he had a vision which revealed the exact time his Master would pass away, and from that moment he was filled with apprehension. He told us time and time again that he did not have one moment of respite; it was a period of constant pain and anguish at the thought of separation. The path he trod was strewn with the pearls of his tears, and they were shed in plenty.

Sant Kirpal Singh would often tell us that it was a great blessing to see one's own Master within, but to have the physical presence of the Master had its own special beauty. During the lifetime of Hazur, the Beloved Master was always yearning to be with him, yearning to gaze into his God-intoxicated eyes. And after Hazur left, we have all seen the depth of his sorrow; even during satsang whenever he talked of Hazur Maharaj Ji, tears would roll down his cheeks. His heart would melt and pour out through his eyes; and these tears would sometimes fall in such profusion that I wrote this verse:

> *Flowers have rained on earth in the form*
> *of tears of love;*
> *Let those who gather them be blessed.*

As I have said, every joy has a hidden sorrow in it. When our Master was with his Beloved Hazur he was intoxicated, lost in his Master's lyrical glances. He was living in eternity. All consciousness of time and space was lost. But with all this there would come the thought, the feeling, "Oh, Master will one day leave me, and all this will stop and only pain will remain." The moment he thought of his Master disappearing from his physical eyes, again that spark of fire which the presence of his Master had cooled, flared up with the winds of apprehension of eventual separation. And so he would be in torture all over again.

Such is the fate of a true lover. Our sweetest songs are those which tell the saddest tale. Bliss is there, but pain is also there. Love is a strange union of the two. Whether it is a period of search through which we are passing, a period of discipleship, or even thereafter, pining and pain will always be ours. That is the basis of mysticism. An Urdu poet has said:

> *A world of people with their heads on*
> *their palms, and a universe of lovers*
> *with their hearts in their hands*
> *are coming to Thy threshold to*
> *lay down their lives at Thy Feet.*

The path of love is a path of sacrifice; it is a path on which we have to undergo much suffering to get that taste of divine love. Even when the Beloved Master started his own ministry he had to face such great trials and tribulations that we can have no idea of their intensity. Although he started with almost nothing, he kept aloft the torch of spirituality handed to him by his Master. Out of his love for us he toiled twenty-two hours a day—sometimes even twenty-four hours a day. He listened to our questions, answered our letters, consoled us, traveled to see us, and all the time he would relieve us of our pain and suffering. He took over so many of our karmas, and he suffered physically for us. Such was his love.

To be purified, gold has to pass through fire before it is free from dross. It is only by passing through various fires that we too become purified. These are the fires of longing for the Beloved, of yearning and pining for the Beloved, even to the point of death. In a state like this how can you be happy? What will be your condition? You will be physically with the Master for short periods, but the periods of separation will seem longer and longer. You will feel that the path you are treading is one of eternal struggle, of endless tears, of pearls flowing from your eyes.

Although I was the most undeserving one, still for reasons, best known to them, both Hazur Baba Sawan Singh and the Beloved Master Sant Kirpal Singh were exceptionally affectionate, loving and kind to me. Hazur was always generous with his love. When I was a child, he would address me as "Kaka" (dear child), "Purana yar" (a friend known from past lives), "Gentleman," or "Darshi." I can still remember—and when I remember this my heart jumps with joy—that he would pat me on my cheeks and then talk to me. He warmly appreciated the verses I wrote inspired by him, and would encourage me in every possible way. So for an undeserving soul who had enjoyed the affection and unbounded grace of both the Masters simultaneously for a quarter of a century, to lose the blessing of even one was a great tragedy. Thus, when Hazur left us it was a great catastrophe in my life, and when it happened it was like experiencing doom. But it was again Hazur's blessing that he provided me relief, and the relief was in the form of the life-inspiring glances, the limitless compassion, love and affection of his successor, the Beloved Master, Sant Kirpal Singh. But even that was only a relief; it could never become a cure, because I had been deprived of the physical darshan of Hazur. After the physical departure of our Beloved Master in 1974, an era of constant torture began for me, for even that relief was gone.

Even though the lover suffers greatly on the spiritual path, Sant Kirpal Singh always said, "Go jolly." We have to keep up our spirits. We should not be overcome with feelings of despondency, disillusionment and disappointment. This is a path of hope; it is a positive path. It is the path lit by the compassion and grace of the Master. It is not a path of darkness. There are moments when we might seem lost, hopelessly lost, struggling through a dark patch, but the eternal torch held by the Master comes to show us the way. We should never lose our spirits. We must always keep up our morale; our soul must stay elevated. And that can be done only if we go jolly. Going jolly means basking in the sunshine of the Master's grace and compassion. We will feel rejuvenated at every step by his divine Light.

This path of love is not so easy as one may think. We have to surrender ourselves completely to the Beloved. When one of the great Persian mystic poets was ordered to be beheaded, he called out to the executioner who was sharpening his sword, "Hasten, dear friend! Come quickly, for I see in your sword the face of my Beloved. With a single blow I shall become one with Him." A true lover endures all suffering and transcends it. He sees the hand of his Master in everything. To be a true lover is a rare gift of God.

Only a few gifted hearts are picked

for playing the melody of love.
It is not a melody which can be
played on every instrument.

CHAPTER TWENTY-FOUR

TWO TYPES
OF
LOVE

*I have loved Thee with two types
of love—one selfish, and the
other worthy of Thee.
As for the first, when I sit in Thy
remembrance, I want Thee all to
myself to the exclusion of others.
As for the one which is worthy of
Thee, therein Thou lift the veil
that I may see Thee.*

Rabi'a Basri, the great mystic woman saint, explains
in this verse that love is of two kinds. One is the selfish
type expressed by the feeling: "I want to be in exclusive
possession of my Beloved; I wish to own the Master. I
want to close my eyes and capture the Beloved within
them. I will not allow any other man or woman to have
a glimpse of my Beloved's resplendent form, nor will I
allow my Beloved to look at anyone else. In this way I
can enjoy the glimpses of the Beloved myself." But she
then goes on to explain that this is a very narrow view, a
wrong path, and the sooner we realize this, the better.

This type of love involves a path of selfishness and possessiveness, and is not the path of mysticism.

She then describes the second type of love: "I shall share my Master's love with the entire world, and not only the souls in this world, but with all the souls in the next one also. The Master's treasures of love never decrease. The more he gives, the more his storehouse increases." This attitude is an expression of universal love. It is the real love of the Master which can be bestowed on each soul in the creation.

We are treading on the path of love, the path of spirituality. Master owns such untold fountainheads of spirituality and love that he can bestow these gifts on each one of us. A Master can love everybody. He can give each one the maximum amount of love that soul can absorb and still his storehouse increases. Whatever amount of love the Master bestows on the people of this world and the hereafter also, it does not decrease the total amount in his reserve. The Master's treasure house of love is endless, and is ever increasing.

The Masters always plead that there should be no jealousy between lovers of the Master, but unfortunately we often suffer from this affliction. It is a fall on the path of love to think that, "If my Master loves somebody else, my share of love will be decreased," or, "If I am not able to possess my Beloved in fullness, then my share may be taken by others." Our path is not one of jealousy. Once we start on this path with instincts of jealousy and envy, then we find ourselves in a sad, morose and pitiable plight. We lose precious ground. And the worst part is that we feel unhappy and wretched only because of our own misunderstanding of the path. If it is necessary for us to sacrifice something in order to move forward to the attainment of our goal, we do not mind sacrificing it. But in this case, we will not sacrifice our wrong way of thinking, and we cause our own torture, despondency and sadness. We spin this web of torture ourselves and end up being caught in it.

We are undergoing the torture of jealousy because of our own narrow angle of vision which is limited to the world of physical love. In that world no one can give the full measure of his love to more than one person. As a result of our narrow vision we are equating love with lust, and the result is we experience self-inflicted pain, trials and tribulations. But if we rise above lust and enter the domain of love, the domain of mysticism and spirituality, then our outlook is transformed. If we understand the basis of mystic love we will begin to go jolly on the path, and our despair and dismay will be reduced to the minimum possible extent.

The basic principle we have to realize is that the Master is not like anyone in this world. We usually think, "Well, this man has a limited treasure—if he gives me something then his riches are reduced by that amount." And we all fear that if he gives some riches to someone else, then our own share will be lessened. But this is a mistaken view. If we want to experience tranquility and ecstasy in their fullness, it is necessary to have the broadest vision. We must begin to realize that the Master has limitless treasures of Naam or Word, and endless gifts of love. We do not understand what boundless Power has blessed us. If he were to distribute the maximum possible love to one and all, to the fill of all the souls in this universe and the next, even then his storehouse would not decrease, but would increase many more times its original size. So why should we have any jealousy toward anyone else?

In many religions, it is considered pious to circumambulate shrines and temples. Khwaja Hafiz, in one of his verses, describes how the Kingdom of God itself is revolving around the lane of the Beloved. The poet wonders how marvelous must be the Beloved around whose threshold God Himself moves. In other words, even God has fallen in love with the Master. Imagine what a great attraction the Beloved has! Our own Beloved Master, Sant Kirpal Singh, also expressed this idea: "My Master is enchanted with God, and God is completely absorbed in my Master."

So this is a path of expansion, and also contraction. From our self we have to expand our love to our family, then to our friends and community, then from our community to the state level, the national level, the international level, the universal level, and ultimately to God Himself. On the other hand, this is also a path of contraction where God, who is limitless, contracts and becomes fully absorbed and manifested in the form of the Master. Can we ever think of becoming jealous of God if He falls in love with the Beloved? And how can we blame our Beloved if he falls in love with God, and through God, with His creation? Can you call your Beloved faithless because he responds to the call of the Creator? If we cannot think of becoming jealous of God, how can we extend jealousy to the poor disciples who have also fallen in love with the Beloved? So jealousy has no place in the spiritual sphere; there is no justification for its existence.

Jealousy on this path is often the result of our misconception of what it is to be alone with the Master. When we see others working with the Master and they are physically close to him, we say to ourselves, "How lucky they are!" And we give ourselves up to envy. The truth is that in attending to his day-to-day work the Master may give his attention to one or the other of his staff for very short periods of time. But he is uninterruptedly with us when he is delivering a satsang, or sitting on the dais during one of the special public functions. We can be with him for two hours and on special occasions for as many as ten or twelve hours.

When we are sitting with the Master, even amongst thousands, we can derive the maximum benefit by learning to capture him within our eyes. When we stop thinking about others, and only think about the Master, we begin to receive his love glances, and once we get those glances of grace we become self-oblivious. Who then remains to wonder whether the Master is looking at others, or even whether he is looking at us! Then, a state arrives as described in two of my verses:

> *O friend, O companion,*
> *Please tell me what my Beloved looks like.*
> *For I have become so lost in my Beloved's*
> *glimpses that my senses fail.*

> *I was so lost in searching for the Beloved;*
> *I did not see the Beloved pass by my side*
> *many a time.*

If we stop thinking of others and only think of the Master, he will shower his divine life-inspiring glances upon us all the time. Think of him alone and sit with him! If Newton could be alone with his problems on the roadside and have no awareness that a band of musicians had passed him, then why can't we be alone with our Master? Newton was alone with his problems, and we can be alone with the solver of our problems. You may be amongst thousands, but even then you can be alone with him.

The Master has equal love for all his disciples. He desires to give his glances to all. But each disciple benefits only in direct proportion to his own receptivity. This accounts for the variations in the rate of progress of those on the spiritual path. If everyone was receptive to the Master, then everyone would be in perfect ecstasy. And if everyone was unreceptive to the Master, then everyone would have to plod slowly on the way. It is a question of plodding on the way or moving at a supersonic speed, and the difference depends on the receptivity of the disciple.

In coming on the spiritual path we sacrifice so much for the sake of love. I have always said how unfortunate it is that those who come in search of the Universal Beloved often become so lost in petty rivalries that they cannot take a step on the path Homewards. Rather, they move in the opposite direction. In one of Tulsi Sahib's verses, he explains the quintessence of spirituality. He says that after deeply exploring everything in this world he has come to the conclusion that there are only five real pearls, and one of them is the *sadh-sangat*, which means the company of our fellow disciples. So disciples of the Master should always have love for each other and help each other. We can help each other to absorb the attributes, glories and beauties of the Master. We can inspire each other to love our Beloved, our Master, with all the intensity of our heart and soul. This is the proper way to approach love on this path. The stranglehold of rivalry and jealousy will lead us nowhere. The Master's path is a path of compassion, grace and lyrical glances. If one of us is lucky enough to have his lyrical glances, then we should emulate that person's virtues, and pray for the Master's glances ourself. Love, if we analyze it, is an attribute of God, while rivalry and jealousy are attributes of the mind, and we have to control them. They should be banished from our vocabulary, banished from our lives. The path of jealousy should be removed from the abode of the Beloved; it is out of place in the Kingdom of Love. The Master is all love; in his domain, there is only a place for true love and true lovers.

CHAPTER TWENTY-FIVE

RUNNING COMMENTARY
OF THE
MIND

Divine, ecstasy-producing music is playing within us ceaselessly. Bliss and peace await us within. Yet what is it that prevents us from enjoying these gifts? It is only our own mind. Instead of listening to the Celestial Harmony we listen to the running commentary of our mind. If we listen to the commentary of a cricket match we hear the commentator saying excitedly: "He hits the ball very hard, and the fielder has not been able to stop it, and it has crossed the boundary and he takes four runs." Similarly, our mind has a running commentary which keeps us from deriving benefit from the Master, from our meditation, from the satsang, and from selfless service.

If we examine the nature of the mind we will find out why it keeps us from progressing spiritually. As our soul is of the same essence as God, mind is of the same essence as Brahm. Brahm's function is to keep the lower worlds going and to see that no soul escapes from his control. So long as souls remain in his control they continue revolving in the cycle of 8.4 million species of life. The mind, which is of Brahm's essence, tries to distract us from progressing on the spiritual path. It tries to distract us from our goal and gets us engrossed in the external world of senses and illusion. The soul meanwhile has the desire to go inward to the spiritual realms.

Thus two governments are being run simultaneously within us—the positive system trying to take us to God, and the negative system or negative power which tries to keep us in the outer world. The mind is no small thing. It is strong and does its best to entangle us in one temptation or the other, and this human life is strewn with temptations at every step. While we are in the human body, our soul and mind are interwoven. Both become subjected to the senses and illusion of the world. The senses of sight, audition, taste, touch and smell are so strong they attract our attention outside. We become identified with the body, and the result is we forget that we are soul, and not the body. It is not an easy task to separate the soul from the body. Mind is like a thousand-headed cobra which plays all sorts of tricks to keep us from gaining right understanding. It is said that Lord Krishna domesticated the thousand-headed cobra—the mind—with the Music of the flute. And that flute is the divine Sound we listen to at the fourth stage, beyond Brahm. It is the living Master who can put us in contact with the divine Sound, and help us rise above body-consciousness. We then realize our body is only a rented house which we have to vacate as soon as the final call comes. The Master helps us to separate our soul from our mind, body and illusion. We can then regain full consciousness.

Even after finding a living Master, and embarking on the spiritual journey, difficulties arise because of the mind's waywardness. Our soul wants to fly into the heavens, and our mind wants to keep us chained to this world. It has many tricks to enchain us. It keeps us from our meditation; it fills us with pride of power, knowledge, and wealth; it makes us think we are above the Master and causes us to judge him on the basis of our own limited understanding; it keeps the mental commentary going so we cannot derive full benefit from attending satsang; and it fills us with jealousy, ungratefulness and lack of forgiveness. It comes up with all kinds of excuses to keep us from doing selfless service. It causes us to camouflage our true selves when we go before the Master. The one object of the mind is to keep us from our spiritual goal.

One of the many blessings of the Master is satsang. Literally "satsang" means "company of truth" or "the company of a saint." We popularly use the word when we refer to the discourse of a saint who talks of the Eternal Power and who sings paeans to the one Lord. We may have attended satsang and listened to the discourses of the Master for years, but let us consider how many of us actually *attend* to the satsang. What we do is, while the saint is delivering his discourses our mind acts like a commentator: "Oh, this is from the holy Bible," and "That has come in the holy Koran," and "This is in accordance with the tenets of the Gurbani," and "This I have not read anywhere so it may be correct or incorrect." How then can we benefit from the satsang? Where is the "company of truth"? Where is the "company of the Master"? Instead, we are keeping company with our own mind! Satsang then becomes a misnomer. Real satsang means communing with the Lord, with the Eternal, with Truth. We may be listening to the satsang with our ears, but true listening is done with the heart. In real satsang we are oblivious to our outer surroundings; we do not know who is sitting to the right of us, to the left of us, to the front or the back of us. If we are completely lost in the Master, and have created a bridge from heart to heart, from eyes to eyes, and from soul to soul, then we are really attending satsang. Then, his every word becomes a part of our lives. If we create that blissful atmosphere, then we can control our mind because we are lost in a Supreme Power. Then, as liquid flows from a higher level to a lower one, so too, the godly qualities of the Master flow into us and gradually replace our worldly qualities. Our vices are replaced with virtues. Our ego, anger and attachment are replaced by humility, love, and selfless service. And if we attain such a sublime state, then we automatically control our mind.

To help us progress and stay out of the clutches of mind and ego, the Master may also bestow on us the gift of selfless service. Although he initiates us and explains how we can attain our goal, how will we become purified enough to progress? We can be purified only when we withdraw our attention from our senses, from our desires. Normally our mind spends all its time thinking about gratifying one physical sense or the other. But the time we spend in selfless service is time spent in remembrance of the Master; it is time we save from thinking about our outer senses. This selfless service is sent to us as a gift from the Master. Through

selfless service we get his blessings, and more and more
of his grace and goodwill. And it is the Master's grace,
it is the Master's joy which ultimately helps us to overcome our mind. The time one spends doing selfless
service is time subtracted from falling prey to the outer
sensations, lusts and temptations of the world. Selfless
service is like a cash crop, the benefits of which can be
immediately reaped during our meditation when we receive an inner boost.

Yet with all these blessings from the Master, our
mind and ego continue to prevent us from gaining
maximum benefit. If we get any progress inside, or if we
are doing selfless service, the ego wants to take credit
for it. It plays its tricks at every step. Talk to somebody
who is full of ego. Even if you mention selfless service,
the moment you touch the strings of the lyre of his
heart, the music of his attainments and sacrifice starts,
and he says, "I have done so much—I have brought
about so many satsang centers; I have brought about
the meeting of such and such person with the Master; I
have gathered so many devotees on the path; I am
mainly responsible for the mission in this country or
that country, or this center or that." Those who are
imbued with humility do not talk tall about their
spiritual progress, or about their sacrifice on the path,
or what they have done for the Master's cause. They do
not cry from the housetops whenever they get a little
experience within—they keep it a secret. Those who
make real progress on the inner way are unassuming
people. All who make tall professions about their
spiritual progress, who boast of their achievements on
the divine path, who claim they are the nearest to the

Master, are the victims of ego and vanity. Their claims are not based on reality. It is a wile of the mind that we think too much of ourselves. We say that *we* can work wonders, that we can bring the stars from the heavens if we so desire. We do not look to our own limitations, and we do not recognize that if we are doing something good, it is due to the good graces of God and our Master. Unfortunately, we always take the credit for any good that comes out of us, while we pass on to others the responsibility for our failings.

Our failure to accept our faults and limitations, but at the same time to take credit for all that we think to be good in our lives, leads us to another wile of the mind— lack of gratitude. We are in the bad habit of clamoring for what we have not got. Suppose I want three books, and you get me two of them. If I say, "I am most grateful to you for getting me these books," then you will think, "Oh, he was so happy to receive the books I gave him, let me also get him the third one." But if instead of thanking you I ask, "Why haven't you brought the third book?" you will think, "He does not even acknowledge the two books I have given him. Let him get the other book himself." If we peep into our hearts we will find that we are seldom grateful to anyone. It is customary to say, "Thank you," for every little thing, but those words only come from our lips, they do not come from our heart. We are all masters of platitudes, but platitudes have no real meaning. It is ultimately that which comes from the core of the heart which affects our very being. We look mostly to the debit side of what others do for us. If a friend has helped us on nine occasions, and on the tenth he is not up to our expectations, we immediately say, "This man is no friend; he never helps me." And when someone is helpful, even then we often think he must have helped us because he wanted to repay something we have done for him, or so he could expect some favor from us in the future. Even in our relationship with the Lord we lack gratitude. We are always grumbling, "If God had only given us more wealth," or "God, why didn't You give us more power and prestige?" We do not appreciate the manifold blessings that God has given us. We do not appreciate that God has blessed us with our very life, with this human form which is the crown of creation. We complain, "God has not given us this thing, He has not given us that thing." But we never speak of all that He *has* given us. It is because of our ego that our vision is so distorted. When we develop humility and gratitude, then we begin seeing things in their true perspective.

We must pray to the Master to grant us the boon of humility. If the disciple at any stage feels that he is equal to the Master, or even better than the Master, it spells his own doom. That is the greatest illusion to which a disciple can fall victim. A disciple who thinks he is better than the Master, is relegating the Master to a position less than what he himself is, and that means being less than even a perfect man! Such thinking stops the disciple's spiritual progress. It makes him an object of ego and vanity. If instead of being humble and grateful we exploit the Master, sit in judgment over the Master like a Solomon, the natural result is that we tumble headlong down. Ego and vanity then lay before us a path of constant delusion and suffering until we again receive the grace of the Master and are able to rid ourselves of these two wiles of the mind.

History is replete with examples which illustrate what happened to disciples who were full of ego and vanity. Tulsidas has an instructive story about a crow in his Hindi epic *Ram Charitra Manas*. A certain crow was able to speak very intelligibly about divinity and how to rise above body-consciousness. The crow was once asked how he gained such divine knowledge and how he was able to discourse with such wisdom. The crow related his tale of woe. He explained that in his previous life he was a disciple. Although his Guru was kind and compassionate to him and taught him the inner knowledge, he was full of ego and vanity, and he grew jealous of his Guru. One day he was in the presence of both his Guru and Lord Shiva, and instead of paying obeisance to his own Guru, he only paid obeisance to Lord Shiva. His Guru, being all compassion, did not mind. But Lord Shiva, as the upholder of justice, got terribly annoyed. He reprimanded the disciple and then cursed him: Because the disciple was disrespectful to his Guru, the disciple would have to be reborn in the form of a snake. The Guru immediately interceded and said, "All children commit mistakes, please forgive him." But Lord Shiva was firm and said, "If I do not maintain order in the world, who else will? I can overlook almost anything, but not a disciple who disowns his Guru, and is jealous of him. My curse will stand."

A true Guru does not mind whether he is insulted, whether he has to go to great trouble for his disciple, whether he has to suffer the greatest possible torture to spare his disciple—his role is to always protect the disciple. So the Guru continued interceding, and as a result Lord Shiva ultimately agreed to change his original sentence. He said that instead of being reborn as a snake, the disciple would have to be reborn as a crow. When the Guru interceded yet again, Lord Shiva said, "My sentence cannot be changed in its entirety because I am duty-bound to maintain discipline and order. However, I will change it to the extent that although he will have the outer form of a crow, he will retain the divine wisdom that you have given him."

Whatever knowledge a disciple may have, whatever accomplishments he may have attained, he should never fall prey to his ego and think that he is greater than his own teacher.

Not only does our ego prevent us from revealing to others our true colors, it even keeps us from being open and honest with our own Master. It has become a way of life with us to put on a camouflage every morning, and to prepare a new face every time we meet a new person. Unfortunately when we go to the Master we carry forward the same technique. What generally happens is, when we meet the Master and he asks us, "How are your meditations?" we say, "Sir, it is all your grace." And when we look into our own heart we find that when we say that, what we really mean is, we have not put in a minute for meditation in the last fortnight. Then, if the Master asks us about our meditations while people are around, we are afraid that if we tell him we are not devoting the required time to meditation, the other people who think we are very advanced on the path will hear our reply and our status will be damaged. This is a great trick of the mind. If the

Master goes out of his way to ask us something we must be bold enough to face him and tell him what our true condition is.

One of the greatest trickeries of the mind is when we say to ourself, "Because Master is all-knowing, why should we tell him anything or talk to him about anything?" If we think that is the case, then why do we visit the Master in the first place? We go to the Master to resolve all our difficulties. We go to tear off this veil between ourself and the Master. But the mind keeps tricking us, even in the presence of the Master. Our relationship with the Master is unique. It is the purest and the highest relationship. If we are not able to be totally honest with the Master, we only deceive ourself. If we are in a predicament and are undergoing a lot of mental torture, and the Master asks, "How are you?" then we should seize that opportunity to speak to him. If instead we say, "I am okay, Sir. I am fine," what purpose does that serve? We may think, "Why bother anyone with our troubles?" And that reply may be true in the case of anyone else who comes along and asks us how we are. But if someone who has love and sympathy for us asks us about our troubles, we should unburden ourself to him. And the Master is such a friend, the most true friend, the only one who can really help us.

Then again, the mind plays another trick telling us, "The Master's time is too precious; I should not waste his time with my problems." If we really feel the Master's time is so precious, then why don't we just stay at home and pray to the Master within? The Master will, of course, look after us wherever we are, but why not take advantage of his physical presence? If we are fortunate enough to be with the Master, we should make the most of the opportunity. If something is preying on our mind and has become a hindrance to our meditations, we must tell the Master about our predicament. The Master can give us special attention which will enable us to improve our meditations. And this is, after all, the real reason we go to the Master. We go to the Master so that if we are not progressing on the path, we can start moving. And if we are already moving on the path, we can accelerate our progress.

Yet another wile to which we fall prey is when the mind tells us, "If we ask the Master a question, it shows a lack of faith in him." If we have any real difficulty we must ask the Master about it, and the Master will reply to such questions. The purpose of being with the Master is to resolve our problems and our doubts. But those doubts should be genuine; they should not be mere intellectual wranglings. Generally, we are not prepared to take the first real step on the path, and yet we ask about the final step. Our soul has not even begun to withdraw from our feet, and we only want to talk about what is going to happen in our Eternal Home, Sach Khand. We can always approach the Master to clarify doubts relating to our present position, and then we should try to progress from that point.

With so many tricks put forth by the mind, how is the poor disciple to overcome his ego? The mind is indeed a bar to our progress, but it can also be a help. The saints have said that the mind is not really our enemy. We have to befriend our mind and put it on the right path. The mind is on the wrong track, but does not know it. Just as our soul is oblivious of its own true glory, our mind also has no idea of its true position. When our soul is elevated, then the mind also is elevated. When our soul transcends the physical plane and goes to the astral plane, our mind also goes there. And when our soul rises to the causal plane, our mind meets its own source, Brahm. So the mind is actually our partner, our fellow traveler through the initial stages of the spiritual journey.

Although our mind tries to entice and entangle us in every possible way so that we deviate from the path, we have to deal with it with love. It is no doubt presently wild and uncontrollable, but like a wild horse, it can be domesticated, and then it can even be useful to us. How can we domesticate the mind? through the Light of God and the Music of the Spheres. When the mind finds a greater attraction and more bliss within, naturally it gives up its desire for the transitory pleasures of the world.

But the mind does not want us to even begin the spiritual journey. It is ensnared in the lower pursuits and tries to entangle us along with it. So in the beginning we have to woo the mind, induce it, persuade it, and cajole it to accompany us on the path. In the initial stages we find that the mind is too strong for us to overcome unaided. We need the help of a living Master so we can control our mind and ego. He helps us by enabling us to rise above body-consciousness and traverse the inner planes. Once we transcend the causal plane, we bid farewell to the mind. Then, we continue our journey until we ultimately merge in God.

CHAPTER TWENTY-SIX
GIVING
AND
RECEIVING

We often think that the luckiest disciples, the ones who are deriving the most benefit from the Master, are those who receive the most time and the most outer attention from the Master. But the spiritual benefit one receives is something which cannot be measured by what we see outwardly. The fact is that the luckiest disciples, the ones who get the best out of the Master, are the ones who have receptivity.

To illustrate this point let me use the example of a teacher. Suppose the teacher has thirty students: Some are turbulent and do not obey the teacher, some are intelligent, some are dull, and some even lack proper development. Out of these children, to whom does the teacher give his best? If we ask any teacher, we find he gives the most time and attention to the worst students, the naughtiest ones, the ones who do not listen to him. To an observer it may appear that the teacher is giving his best to these students, but in reality, the teacher is only *trying* his best with them—he is not *giving* his best to them. There is a difference between trying to be helpful and giving your best. The child who is the worst might get the most time and attention, but he may not get the best benefit out of the teacher. Who will get the best benefit? the most obedient and responsive pupil. A teacher gives his best to somebody who is able to receive the best from him, somebody who is receptive. The question of giving our best has the question of receiving embedded into it. If there is no one who can receive, to whom will we give? When we say we are giving our best to someone we imply that there is someone at the receiving end, someone who is receptive. Giving and taking go hand in hand.

For anyone to master a subject, a bridge has to be built between the teacher and the taught. It is only after the bridge has been built that the attributes and qualities of the teacher begin to flow in the direction of the student. But if the bridge has not been built, if the child is not receptive, what is the teacher to do? There are then only two choices: One is to leave the difficult child in the lurch, but that is not a quality of a good teacher. The second alternative is to work hard against all odds, and hope for ultimate success. If the teacher fails, at least he has the satisfaction of having done his best. Sometimes it happens that the love and attention of a teacher convert the most obstinate student and change his entire pattern of life. And that is where the teacher achieves his or her acme of success. In comparison to the more difficult students, the responsive ones may get less time and less outer attention from the teacher. But in reality, it is they—the receptive ones—who derive the most benefit.

This analogy can also be applied to the Master and

his disciples. Somebody might be in the physical presence of the Master and spend a lot of time with him, but if that person is not receptive, he does not receive the best from him. Someone else may receive the glance of the Master for just a split-second and be transported to the heavens. Let me relate to you an incident from my own life. In college we had three months vacation. I had gone to the Dera in Beas to be with my Master, Hazur Baba Sawan Singh, for three or four weeks. On my last day at Beas, in the afternoon, I went in search of Hazur. But he was nowhere to be seen and no one knew where he was. At about 6:30 p.m. I found someone who knew his whereabouts, but when I finally got to see Hazur, he was very busy. I tried to catch his eye, but somehow or other his glances roamed in all directions except the one in which I was sitting. At first I tried changing my position, but with no better results. So I resigned myself to just sitting there. When Hazur was finished with what he was doing he said, "Kaka, (dear son), you are here?" I said, "Sir, I have to return home." Hazur said, "It is already so late in the evening. How can you go back now?" I replied, "My father has asked me to come back." Hazur asked, "Why does he want you to return? Aren't you still on vacation?" I said, "Sir, there are still three weeks left." Hazur asked, "Did he really ask you to come back?" I replied, "He gave me strict instructions." So Hazur said, "All right, then you must go." I was hoping in my heart that after all those questions Hazur would give me another lease on life. But that was denied. I went with Hazur to his bungalow, and he took me to his room. I put my head on his feet and he patted me, saying, "All right, you go." And then he gave me *prashad* (food blessed by the Master). When we came out Hazur started climbing the stairs, and as I stood at the bottom, I kept looking towards his back. I was, at heart, unhappy about having to leave his physical presence, but I thought, "Orders are orders and they must be obeyed." As Hazur was taking the turn on the flight of stairs, he looked at me for a split-second—just a split-second! And that gave me such a thrill that when I left the Dera I had the Master's radiant form before me. With darkness all around, I had to walk, carrying my luggage, four miles to the railway station. But Hazur's form was always with me. I bought my train ticket and found that he was with me. I could see his physical form with me all the time. He was with me even when I was in the bathroom! When I read I would see Hazur and not the book. With open eyes I was seeing him all the time. This condition continued for some days. I could not study because I was always seeing Hazur, even when I tried to read a book. And this experience was a result of a split-second glance! For a very long period the Sound Current continued so strongly that I would sometimes not be able to hear people who were with me. Some people said I was absentminded; others thought that my entering a prestigious college had turned my head, but in reality I was not hearing them, I was hearing only the Sound Current. So time is no measure of our receiving the grace of the Master. Even a split-second glance of the Master can pierce and permeate our whole being.

We can be sitting alone at home, in any country of the world, and can be in the company of the Master if we are remembering him, if we are talking to him

within, if we are lost in him, if we are receptive. The
Master is not somebody who is living in a certain
locality, in a certain building. He is not a single physical
entity. In the Shabd form, he is everywhere. He
multiplies himself into the number of people he has to
look after and he can be with each one of his disciples at
the same time. To the naked eye it appears that he is
talking to one person, but if he wants he can know at
the same time everything that is happening to each
individual within his circle of grace. He may be talking
to any one of us, and at the same time he might be taking another man out of the body, and helping all his
other children according to their own needs. All initiates
can enjoy the ecstasy of the love glimpses of the Master
wherever they are because the Master is always sitting
within them and watching them. If they are receptive,
they can commune with the Master wherever they are.
Our love for him should be so strong that we are in
direct contact with him via the wings of our love.

If we have the good fortune of being with the Master
we should sit in his presence with our whole being—we
should become one big eye and one big ear. If we are receptive, then we are not aware of anyone else. If we are
receptive, then even if we are with him for a short time,
we will be in bliss—in a state of eternity. But if we are
constantly aware of the presence of others, if we are
constantly mindful of what others are saying and how
others are behaving, then even a lifetime spent in the
physical presence of the Master is in reality being away
from the Master's presence.

A few lucky people learn the secret of receptivity,
and they carry the Master locked in their eyes, in their

heart and in their soul. They can be in their home, in an orchard, or under a tree. They can be on the bank of a river, or under the starry skies, or in the sun-scorched desert. Wherever they are they remain in the Master's presence, and it is they who derive the most benefit.

CHAPTER TWENTY-SEVEN
NINE SIGNS
OF A
LOVER

We all claim to be lovers of God. We speak eloquently about the pangs of separation, about our longing and pining, about our yearning to be with the Beloved. We make endless professions of love to our Beloved and express in a thousand ways that we are true lovers, that our love and sincerity are constant. Scanning through books of poetry and written music, we find imagery to reveal our intense craving and desire for the Beloved. We claim that the intensity of our love is increasing every moment, and if the Beloved does not respond, then the strings of the lyre, the strings of our heart are going to break. We profess our constancy, and hope that the Beloved will have mercy on us.

Despite our professions, in reality we do not have this intensity of love, we do not possess this constancy of love. We go on repeating that we are filled with true love, but our actions prove that we are not only insincere to our Beloved but we are insincere to ourself. We hide our true feelings. What we say is not true, it is only a profession. Our emotions, our own experiences, are not depicted in their true perspective. We want to show that our love is so great that we would live and die for our Beloved, but in reality we only live and die for our own self. We show off, and only assume a camouflage of being a true lover, of having constancy, sincerity, and faithfulness in our love. This is our way of life these days, this is the way of life of the modern world.

We talk about the great achievements of man, and our spectacular progress in the technological and the scientific realms. But so far as our souls are concerned, we have moved from the sublime to the ridiculous. We have moved from the age of chivalry to the age of self-indulgence, from the age of discipline to the age of disorder. We have moved from cosmos to chaos, and from sublimity to selfishness—to naked selfishness. This is the so-called progress that we have made.

We are all in search of God in one way or the other, and for this, we need to know who the true lovers of God are. If we wish to search for God we must find a true lover, for it is only from a true lover that we ourself can develop love for God. You can see why, in our modern world, it is so imperative that we know how to discriminate between a true lover and a false one, how to differentiate and distinguish between an embodiment of sincerity and faithfulness, and an embodiment of outward show and fickle-mindedness.

In this context, the Sufis have described nine signs of a true lover of God. These nine signs will lead you to kingly light. They will give you a touchstone that you can apply to find out whether the so-called lover is in reality a true lover. True lovers are neither egoists nor egotists. They are unassuming, simple people. These nine signs of a lover which I will try to explain are given in the mystic scriptures.

The first sign of a lover is that he heaves cold sighs. When you have some aching pain in your heart, when you are leaving the Beloved, you heave cold sighs. You are in a forlorn state: You are pining and longing for your Beloved, you are yearning for your Beloved. When everyone has left you, when you are deserted and you find that your Beloved is even keeping her shadow away from you, you heave cold sighs. When you feel that you have no one to care for and remember you, when you have no one to keep you company, when you are left in the lurch all by yourself—in that state you heave cold sighs.

During the times you have the warmth of your Beloved's thoughts, you feel some life in you. When you have even the slightest idea that your Beloved loves you at heart, but because of certain reasons is forced by outer circumstances to show indifference, even then you have some warmth in your heart. Your very life is sustained by the warmth produced by the love of the Beloved. But when you start feeling that your Beloved has severed all connections with you, when you feel that warmth is gone, then your sighs become cold.

This first sign is the greatest test because the heart of the lover is likely to flutter. The lover is caught in the tresses of the Beloved, and this stage of cold sighs is sometimes apt to lead the lover to a state of despair and despondency. And in that semi-lunatic state the bird of the heart flutters in its cage of trials and tribulations. Once caught, this bird of the heart cannot become free again. In spite of its fluttering and crying, once a captive, it is a captive for all times. The lover needs all the sympathy, all the pity for his helpless state. He now feels hopeless and abandoned because there is no one to care for him. The lyrical glances and the love that emanate from the Beloved are no longer felt. The lover is in a pitiable state of cold sighs. In Christian mysticism this period is referred to as "The dark night of the soul."

The second sign of a lover is his pale color. You will not find a lover with rosy cheeks, because rosy cheeks only belong to the Beloved. Poetically, the rose face and the tulip face are the monopoly of the Beloved. A lover only has a pale face and there is a reason for this. It is said that if you happen to cut the veins of a lover you will not find any blood flowing through them; you will find that only love is flowing through them. So the redness of the blood is gone from the face of the lover, and the paleness of his love is portrayed on it.

The pale yellow-colored flower called the narcissus is often compared to a lover in mystic poetry. It is called the "patient," one who is ailing, suffering from the malaise of love. As a result, this pale yellow flower is known as the ailing narcissus. And the malady of love is such that once we are infected, we can never find a cure for it. The lover may be in the elementary stages of this malaise, or he may be in the advanced stages when his life itself threatens to ebb away. So the second sign of a lover is that he will have a pale complexion because he is always infected with the sickness of love.

The third sign of a lover is moist eyes. The lover has to undergo the pangs of separation from the Beloved.

One of my verses is:

Even if we have caught some stray
moments of bliss, they were only
transitory,
But the sorrows that fell to our share
were lasting.

It is the unfortunate lot of a lover to go on pining and yearning for the Beloved. This is a path of continuous suffering. And as a result of this continuous suffering our heart melts and gushes up to the eyes in the form of moisture. But this path of love must also be a path of self-control, because love is the secret of secrets. Love is a secret between the lover and the Beloved. It should not be revealed to any third person. If it is revealed to anyone, then it is no longer love; it is only an exhibition of love. So there is another pitiable plight of the lover. Tears gush out from the heart and come up to the eyes; they come up to the eyelashes, but never appear on the eyelashes. If they flow onto the eyelashes, then this secret is revealed, and it is no longer a secret. It becomes an exhibition of our love, and creates a tumult. People will gather around and ask you why you are crying, and what has happened.

So lovers have to be disciplined. Their tears come up to the eyes, but lovers have to control and contain them in the sockets of the eyes. The sockets of the eyes become like an oyster. Priceless pearls are formed inside the oyster. According to poetic traditions, it is not the ordinary seawater which flows in and out of the oyster that produces pearls. A special rainwater, a special ambrosia from the heavens, passes through the mouth of the oyster and goes to its base where it is nourished for a long time before it takes on the form of a pearl. But the ordinary water which flows in and out of the oyster always remains water. Similarly, if a tear comes into the socket of the eye, which is like an oyster, and flows out of the eye, it remains water. But if you control your tears, if you seal them inside, if you give them life inside, if you nourish them with your love, if you feed them with your molten heart, then they become pearls. Yes, this is a path of tears, but it is a path of tears which are hidden from the public eye; these are tears that are only seen by the inner eye of our anguished soul.

The fourth sign of a lover is that he eats very little. If we have to eat and if we have to drink, we eat our Beloved, and we drink our Beloved. It is not necessary to eat much of the outer foods. We need not worry that we will lose weight, and waste away to nothing, because the love of the Beloved runs in our veins. When we have the love of our Beloved in our veins we are cheerful and jolly with very little food; the Beloved's love becomes our food.

The fifth sign is that the lover talks little. This is not a path of chatterboxes, grumbling-boxes, and complaining-boxes. It is blasphemous to grumble on the path of love. It is a path of the sober ones, a path of the unassuming ones. It is a path of those who sacrifice their lives, but no grumbling ever comes on their lips. One of my verses is, "I intended to grumble to my Beloved, but when I came into his presence the complaint was transformed into a prayer." So complaints and grumbling, both outer and inner, are a sacrilege on this path. Lovers speak very little, and they do not cry out from the housetops whenever they get a little experience within; they keep it a secret within themselves. True lovers do not brag about their sacrifices on the path.

The sixth sign of the lover is sleeplessness: long vigils and sleeping very little. One of my verses is:

> *O, the very life of my dreams and visions,*
> *Whosoever came to Your million-mirrored*
> * sleeping chamber never desired to*
> * go home.*
> *And if he did leave, he left his sleep*
> * behind.*

The imagery in this verse comes from the Moghul period, when the sleeping chambers of the queens and kings had millions of small mirrors on all four walls and on the floor below and the ceiling above. If you saw your beloved in such a chamber, not only did you behold her before you, but you saw her scintillating beauty reflected in the million mirrors surrounding you. And that made such a deep impression on you that you could not leave, because the beauty was so captivating, so enticing. You became a victim to it for all time. And even if you were able to leave, you lost your sleep. When you left the image of pristine beauty, you were constantly longing for that beauty, constantly pining for that beauty. When your desire is so intense to see that beauty again, you cannot sleep, you are bereft of sleep.

So the sixth sign of a lover means that sleep is forbidden to him. And if the lover indulges in sleep he is committing a sacrilege. Sleep suggests that we are indifferent to the object of beauty.

The seventh sign of a lover is restlessness. A lover's

heart is often compared to mercury, which is moving all the time; it never rests even for a second. It is always tossing and turning for the Beloved. And when the heart is restless for the Beloved, one does not find any charm in outer attractions. If you put a restless heart in a luxurious building, it will still be restless. If you give a restless heart the benefit of the latest gadgets, it will still be restless. If you take a restless heart to the moon along with the astronauts, it will still be restless. The restlessness cannot be assuaged by any material object. The restlessness is caused by separation from the Lord of Lords, from the Ocean of All-consciousness. That is why despite our spectacular progress in materialism and science, we are unhappy and our souls are restless. Our souls are a conscious entity, and if anything will give us relief, if anything will give us comfort, it is only coming in contact with All-consciousness, coming to the feet of a conscious entity, a perfect Master. All our mighty achievements in the field of science and materialism cannot give any solace to our restless soul.

Next, we come to the eighth sign which is sorrow. It is a poignant sorrow, a constant sorrow that sometimes is transformed into weeping in torrents. And the torrents that start falling are not tears, but pearls that have been stored in the eyes. When the lover is plunged into the depths of this heartrending sorrow, the only comforter who can stop his tears and soothe his anguished heart is the embodiment of love, the Master.

Finally, the ninth sign is constant cries of the heart, the wailing of the heart. A true lover cries out from the core of his being, from the innermost depths of his heart. And those cries are so poignant, so strong, they have such force in them that they are ultimately heard by the Creator. It is said by Guru Gobind Singh that God listens to the sincere cry from the heart of an ant sooner than He listens to the trumpeting of an elephant. If our cries come from the core of our heart, and they are filled with perfect devotion and perfect sincerity, which are the hallmarks of a true lover, then they are bound to reach God, they are bound to reach our Creator, they are bound to reach the solver of all problems. And God not only listens to them, He is moved by them. And He is not only moved by them, but He also becomes restless. God Himself comes in search of a true lover.

One of my verses is:

When a perfect man cries for the Lord
from the core of his heart,
He becomes the object of God's search.

Man is searching everywhere for God. But God is embedded in our heart. It is a strange paradox that we are looking for God outside. We go from one place of pilgrimage to another. We look for God in the valleys and dales, or on the peaks of the Himalayas. Sometimes we even look for God, the very Water of Life, in the deserts.

God Himself is in search of a perfect man. God Himself is in search of someone having the nine signs of a lover. The cries that come from the core of a disciple's soul, so move God's heart that He descends from the heaven-heavenly to the earth-earthy in search of such a lover. God comes here in the form of the Beloved, in the form of a living Christ, in the form of a living Master. He brings his disciples to his feet, initiates

them, and gives them a contact with the Light of God
and the Music of the Spheres. He teaches the disciple
the art of dying while living, and he enables the disciple
to enter the Kingdom of God by being born anew. He
takes the true lover to the higher regions, and ultimately
to the final stage where the soul loses its identity and becomes one with God. This is the story of the true lover,
the supreme lover, who is a microgod in the beginning
and who becomes God Himself in the end.

CHAPTER TWENTY-EIGHT
CONTINUOUS STRUGGLE

Others are leading a life of goblets
and cups
And are getting intoxicated with cup
after cup of wine served to them;
But I derive my intoxication from the
cold-blooded murder of my desires.

This verse of mine often causes those inexperienced
on the path of mystic love to think this path is one of
tragedy, disaster and catastrophe. To those who think
the purpose of life is only luxury and enjoyment, the
path of love is a thorny one. But this is only because we
do not really know what true love is.

Those steeped in the traditions of the East, those
who are familiar with mystic love, know that a lover
must undergo many trials. Without a grumble they
accept them as the normal lot of a lover. While many
people are apprehensive of the trials and turmoils, the
cruelties and tyrannies which the Beloved inflicts, real
lovers revel in being caught in the coils of the Beloved's
tresses. Those who have experienced being caught in

love know that any attempt to shake off those coils ends in failure. A true lover relishes being a captive of the Beloved's curls and begins enjoying it. It becomes his way of life to experience ecstasy in his seeming captivity, and he surrenders to it.

Have you ever been a victim of Cupid's arrow? If your beloved rejected your advancing gestures, how did you feel? And when you were persistent, and the beloved was only critical of you and committed atrocities upon your heart, and resisted you at every stage, did you not continue to woo her despite her actions? Did you not continue to follow the path of Cupid?

A lover goes to the extent of praying, as I have expressed in one of my verses:

> *Give me but one glance of your love,*
> *And I would be willing to suffer your*
> *cruelties for the rest of my life.*

In order to make progress on the path of love we have to become completely reoriented, we have to have one object in view. A true lover is moved by one thought: how to reach the Beloved, how to woo the Beloved. The lover is prepared to pay any price for his Beloved.

Once you get caught in the tresses of your Beloved, if you make an effort to raise your head out of one noose of the tresses, you will find that your head is then caught in yet a bigger noose. And if you try to break this noose two or three times, after a while you will surrender yourself to your fate. What is more, you will even begin deriving pleasure from it. Just look at a bird who is caught and put in a cage. How he flutters for the first few days. But after a while he settles down. He is tamed. For the first few days he does not take any food or water. Then slowly he starts eating and drinking. After a few weeks, he begins slowly responding to your voice. And finally he begins pouring forth warblings. Such is the condition of a lover who is caught in the tresses of the Beloved.

Once struck by the arrow of love, you are captive forever. What can you do about it? Master has many an arrow of love in his quiver. He can enrapture you with a single glance. He can put you in a state of ecstasy, and then rob you of your heart when you are under a spell. If you can escape one arrow, he has another arrow. He has so many arrows in his quiver. And a poor victim, once caught, is always caught.

These are the hard truths of life. I can express them in very ornamental language. I can express them in platitudes. I can say that the moment you come to a Master you get intoxicated with his eyes, and that intoxication increases every moment until you attain communion with the Lord. If you would like I can describe the path of love in these words but in doing so I would neither be fair to myself nor to you. What I have been explaining is the truth of the mystic path that you do not find in books. Had they written about this in the books with such great clarity, then people would have shunned this path. But this is the naked truth and the only truth. It is a fact that you ultimately enjoy lasting bliss, lasting ecstasy, lasting salvation. Nobody can deny that. But I have explained in detail all of the stages which are full of pain, anguish and yearning so that you should not be afraid of facing these moments on the path. Kabir, Guru Nanak, and all the great mystics have spoken of these moments. Our Beloved Master Sant Kirpal Singh Ji used to say that this is a path of tears; this is a path of dampness. He would say, "When love dances on the heart, it pains. But that pain is coated with honey. Who is there who would give up that pain?" People have been referring to this aspect of the path since the dawn of eternity, but we have not heeded their words. For those on the path of love, the pain and the suffering may be intense, but as Ghalib, the great Urdu poet has said, "When your grief transcends all bounds, it becomes its own cure."

What is not hard on love's way? The trouble is that we do not know what love is. We only think of love in terms of lust, or at the most, infatuation; we do not go beyond that. First, our mind and our soul have to be molded so as to understand what true mystic love is. We have to rise above our limited concept of love and reach a higher understanding. We think of God's love in terms of man's love. We have no conception of real love, of mystic love.

When I was in my first year at college, I had difficulty in understanding the connotations of love in the poetry of the Urdu poet, Sir Muhammed Iqbal. The opening line of one of his ghazals is:

> *There are worlds beyond the stars*
> *and there is many a test of love*
> *which has yet to be undergone.*

Another verse says:

> *It is love which causes the ups and*
> *downs in human life.*

*It is love which brings about the high
notes and low notes in music divine.
It is love which gives an endless boost
to the wayfarer.*

I asked my professor at college what the meaning of these verses was. To my surprise and joy he invited me to accompany him that evening on his visit to the home of the great poet. After my professor told Dr. Iqbal that I wanted to understand the meaning of these verses, the poet looked at me penetratingly for some time and said, "Wherever I have used the word 'love' in my poems, it means a continuous struggle, a never-ending struggle. Try to understand my poetry in the light of this interpretation."

That is how I first came to understand that love is a constant struggle to attain the Beloved, to obtain the cherished object. This constancy involves our whole being and our wholehearted attention. We must accord it the first priority in our life. We must have one ruling thought, one ruling passion, one objective, one destination. Ultimately, the lover becomes lost in the Beloved and it is difficult to know who is the lover and who is the Beloved. At this stage, the lover becomes the Beloved—the lover becomes God Himself.

CHAPTER TWENTY-NINE
SURRENDER

In India there is a fruit known as the jaman which is like a black grape in appearance, but whose taste has a tinge of tartness. In order to bring out its best flavor and give it a touch of sweetness we have a process whereby we fill an earthenware pot halfway with the jamans. We then add some salt, cover the pot and shake it vigorously. When the pot is uncovered and the jamans are placed on a plate, we find some of them look the same as they did before the shaking, but many of them have been split open or crushed. While the taste of each of them is sweeter, some of them have been destroyed in the process. Those jamans which did not withstand the shaking were broken, but those which accepted the treatment and were able to withstand it are enjoyed and cherished for both their beauty and their sweetness.

Similarly, in order to make something of great value and beauty of the lovers, the Beloved sometimes shakes up their hearts. Not all the lovers can withstand it. Many hearts become crushed or broken in this process. But those who are able to submit to the Beloved's

shake-up, and who surrender to it, are not broken—
instead they come out whole and give forth the sweetest
taste. Such lovers who have surrendered to the
Beloved's treatment, be it gentle or vigorous, are the
most fortunate.

In mysticism, self-surrender is the path of placing
ourselves entirely in the hands of the Master, and whatever happens, nothing should shake our faith in him. In
so many spheres of life we surrender ourselves completely, even to worldly beings. In this connection,
Hazur Baba Sawan Singh used to explain that when we
have some physical trouble, we go to a competent
surgeon for help. After he takes all possible tests and x-
rays, he advises us that we need an operation. On his
advice, which is only human advice, we agree to the
operation, and then surrender ourselves completely to
him. Once we have agreed to the operation, we no longer make intellectual judgments, we simply surrender to
whatever the surgeon says and does. We are even asked
to sign a declaration by which we place ourselves entirely in his hands, and are prepared to accept all the
consequences of the operation irrespective of the results. The great Hazur would then say, "You place
yourself entirely in the hands of an ordinary surgeon,
but you do not do so in the case of your Master!" If we
can surrender to a doctor whose job is to cure our
physical body, then why can't we surrender to the
Supreme Doctor who can cure our soul? An aspirant for
spirituality has to make sure about the spiritual
competence of a Master. But after he has taken the decision to follow the Master, he should then submit himself wholly and solely to the Master's direction without

any mental reservations. Only a Master knows the turns and twists on the spiritual path, and he alone is in a position to act as an unerring guide.

There is a famous couplet from a poem by the Persian mystic Hafiz, which illustrates the need for surrender to the Master. Hafiz was a professor in a university in Persia in the fourteenth century. He was renowned for his encyclopedic knowledge and his vast learning. Once he wrote a hemistich, half a verse, (each verse consists of two hemistiches) that said:

> *If your Master orders you to dye your*
> *prayer mat with wine, do so.*

Persia is a Muslim country, and for Muslims wine is strictly prohibited. Anyone who drinks wine is considered by the Muslims to be an infidel, and he is barred from their religious assembly. Just look at the daring of the poet—he not only says to touch wine, but he says that if the Master orders, drench the prayer mat—a most sacred object—in wine! This hemistich resulted in a great outcry in the country, and everybody said Hafiz had become a heretic, and should be punished. The emperor of Persia was duly informed of Hafiz's heretical statement and he asked the caliph to investigate the matter. At that time, legal judgments were made by the caliphs who were masters of Islamic law. Now, the caliph at that time was a very wise man. All sorts of pressure was put on him to execute or flay Hafiz alive, but the caliph had read Hafiz's poetry and had met the great mystic. He knew he could not reach a judgment without first having a proper investigation. The people complained, "What investigation is required? This is a clear case of heresy—execute him." But the caliph withstood all the pressure, went to see Hafiz and said, "I understand that you have written this hemistich: 'If your Master orders you to dye your prayer mat with wine, do so.' Not only has it spread like wildfire, it has also produced fire amongst the listeners. I know in my heart of hearts that there must be some sound basis for the couplet, but I am unable to understand it. Will you kindly clarify it for my sake? On my own I would not have come to investigate this, for I know that when you write the second hemistich everything will be clear, but I have been commanded by the emperor to investigate, and I had to come to you for that." Hafiz said, "I have another mystic friend who lives on a hillock some distance off. First go to him and do what he says, and then when you return to me I will explain the meaning of what I have written." The caliph began having doubts, and thought, "This man has not explained anything. Had this been a clear-cut matter he could have explained the couplet straight away, but since he has not explained it to me, there must be something fishy about it." Nevertheless, he was happy that Hafiz had at least acknowledged having written the controversial hemistich.

As he was traveling to see the mystic who was a friend of Hafiz, he was thinking, "Hafiz is a man with such a crystal-clear mind and his poetry is the finest, but he was not able to reply to me. By sending me to his friend he probably wanted to gain time to make up some story to justify what he has written."

Upon reaching the other mystic, the caliph related the whole story. He then said, "My friend Hafiz said that I should come to you first and follow your instructions. Then, he said, he would expound the true meaning of the hemistich."

The second mystic said in a rather carefree manner, "All right, we will talk about it later." Then he told the caliph to go to the house of a certain prostitute who lived on a certain street in a nearby town. The caliph got the shock of his life, and thought, "What sort of mystics are these? One says to dye your prayer mat in wine, and the other says to go to a prostitute! One outdoes the other at this dirty game!" But since the caliph was under orders from the emperor, he had to carry out the investigation. There was no way out. As he proceeded on his way, he was deeply troubled and his mind was filled with terrible thoughts. He was giving a mental beating to these mystics, calling them heretics, immoral people, and whatever else came to his mind.

When he reached the residence of the prostitute, he was seated in a reception room. While he waited an attendant of the house came and served him food. By now the caliph regretted having come at all. He started shivering in his shoes, thinking, "I am in such a disreputable place. If somebody sees me here, he will say, 'Look at this caliph, what a place he is visiting!' "

In a short while a young damsel entered his room. He noticed that the girl, who was dressed in fine clothes, was perspiring from head to foot, trembling and shaking. "This is not the behavior we normally connect with a prostitute," he thought. "They usually come in either dancing, or in their own coquettish manner to enrapture and entice the heart of the visitor." This set him thinking. The girl walked forward, halting at every step, and trembling more and more. Sensing how nervous she was, he said, "Don't worry, I am not going to touch you. But tell me, how is it that you are in such a plight?" The girl said, "Sir, I am the daughter of a respectable man. When I was very young, robbers came and plundered our street, and carried me along with them. They sold me to the owner of this house, and because the prostitute you have come to see is away today to be with a nobleman, I have been pushed in here to take her place. So far, by the grace of God, I have led a chaste life. I know from the training which I received in my parents' home, and from my own conscience, that this is not the right path. And I would rather die than enter this lane of sin.

The caliph was filled with sympathy, as he remembered that some years back there had been a robbery in his own house, and his young daughter had been carried away by the bandits. Becoming more inquisitive, he asked, "Can you tell me about the town in which you were living?" The girl said, "I am not very clear about it, but the name was something like...." To the shock of the caliph it sounded like the name of his own town. Then he further asked, "Can you tell me the name of the street on which you lived?" She again, depending on her memory said, "I am not very clear but it was something like...." And it resembled the name of his own street. Finally, he asked, "Do you remember the name of your father?" And again she replied in the same way, "Sir, I do not recollect exactly, but it was something like...." At that, the caliph burst into tears as he realized that this was his daughter. He fell on his knees and said, "I am all gratitude to God Almighty that He has sent me here to save your honor."

He immediately contacted the owner of the house and paid her whatever price she wanted for the girl's release. He took hold of his daughter's hand and set off for the hut of Hafiz's mystic friend. Now tears were flowing from his eyes—tears of repentance. He was cursing himself for having doubted the intentions of the mystic. He was cursing himself for being so callous, for being so hasty to pass judgment on these saints. He said, "I have been reading the works of the greatest of these people all my life, and I was led astray with the slightest provocation. I should have been more sensible—I should have exercised a greater degree of restraint over my mind. Why was I so hasty to judge Hafiz? Why have I been cursing such godly people? How can I ever be forgiven for having such evil thoughts when these saints were performing the greatest act of kindness?" In that state of mind the caliph went to the mystic, fell at his feet and said, "I ask for your forgiveness. Apparently, you had sent me to the house of a prostitute, but in reality you sent me to save the honor of my own daughter. We worldly people view everything from our own limited and biased vision. We cannot understand the true meaning of the words of the godly people, and because of this we undoubtedly go wrong." After the caliph shed many tears, the mystic comforted him and said, "It is all right." But the caliph said, "Sir, it is not all right. I hurled so many abuses on you, I had so many doubts about you. I don't know how God is going to forgive me." The great mystic told him, "My dear friend, none of your abuses or bad thoughts have been hurled maliciously, but they were only due to your lack of right understanding. You have my blessings; now forget all about this event.''

Suddenly, remembering his original assignment, he asked, ''What about that hemistich? I had come to you for clarification of the hemistich which I still do not understand.'' And the mystic said, ''Go and ask my friend Hafiz to write the second hemistich and thus complete the verse.''

The caliph went with his daughter to Hafiz. He prostrated himself at the saint's feet and related to him what had happened. He cried and said, ''You are men of God. We are men of mind and matter. You are purity personified. It is we who are sinful. You look at things from a high angle, we look from a very limited vision. Only you know what you are doing. We always misunderstand you. This investigation has been an eye-opener for me. I have learned one thing: Whatever you do, that is the outcome of chastity, piety and godliness.'' He then said, ''Your friend has requested you to complete the verse by adding a second hemistich so that people do not misconstrue your meaning. Hafiz then completed the verse:

The one who guides you is never unaware
of the intricacies and pitfalls of the
path.

Whatever the Master tells us, whatever he does, is in accordance with the highest principles of divinity. It is only we with our limited understanding who cannot appreciate their true meaning. When the verse had been completed, the caliph reported the entire matter to the emperor. The second hemistich was published immediately throughout the country. All the fire and fury died down and was changed into applause and appreciation for the great mystic poet Hafiz.

This is the path of self-surrender. If the Master asks us to dye our prayer mat in wine, we should dye it with wine without asking how or why. But we can only do this when we are fully convinced that our eternal Beloved, our Master, our spiritual mentor, is the Word-made-flesh, that he has become one with the Power of God, and is in fact God-personified. When we begin to personally experience the greatness of the Master, when we experience the Light and Sound of God within, then gradually we gain more and more confidence in our Master, more and more faith in our Master. When a disciple first came to Hazur, the great Master would say, "Take me to be an elder brother, take me to be a teacher, take me to be an advisor, and when you go within, then you can think of me however you like." Conviction is never based on hearsay. It develops over time. But sometimes, just as people experience love at first sight, due to past karmas some people have full trust at first sight. When that conviction is gained, then there is no difficulty. It is only mind, matter and illusion which are the stumbling blocks in the way of our surrendering ourself entirely to the Beloved. Just as we have the conviction that our surgeon is competent and we do not argue with him about which is the best course to adopt when performing surgery, once we have made the decision to come to the feet of a perfect Master, we do not judge intellectually whether the Master's commandments are right or wrong, we do not argue with him about the best course to adopt; we simply surrender ourself to him. Placing ourself entirely in the hands of the Master means cessation of all intellectual wrangling. Surrender implies that we have to carry out his commandments without applying the touchstone of our limited intellect. Now, that is a difficult job because in our day-to-day work in this world we are in the habit of trying to judge everything from our own level of understanding. It is easy to profess that we have surrendered ourself to the Master, but in reality we find that our intellect and our mind are always putting forward some flimsy excuse to keep us from fully surrendering. The moment we start applying our intellect to the Master's commandments, our ego starts playing its own unhealthy part, and that might distract us from the right path for at least a transient moment, if not for a longer period.

We can see some reflection of the meaning of surrender in a mother's love for her child. A mother does not judge what is coming to her from her child. Because she is full of love for the child, she allows him to play as he likes. The child may be putting his fingers into the mouth or nostrils of the mother, slapping the mother, or pulling her tresses, but the mother never becomes offended. In fact, she goes on kissing and embracing the child. When a mother is completely lost in her child, she is in a state of ecstasy, and she allows the little child full play. Does the mother judge the actions of the child with her intellect? She treats the child with all affection, and whatever the child does, the mother not only accepts, she relishes and enjoys. In the same way, a disciple who has really surrendered, relishes whatever comes to him from God, from his Master.

The test of true surrender comes only when we pass through a period of trials and tribulations, and we still go on saying, "Sweet is Thy will." If things are going along all right with our business and family affairs, and everything is going according to our own sweet will, it is easy to say, "I am always grateful to the Master, I always surrender to the Master." But our words have no real meaning. It is only when something goes wrong and we say, "Sweet is Thy will," that our words take on real meaning.

The Beloved Master used to say that when a potter shapes a clay pitcher he always keeps his hand inside the vessel so it does not break while he strikes it into shape from outside. Similarly, when we undergo a difficult period, the Master is always supporting us. If by chance we pass through a period of poverty or ill health, or our public image is spoiled, we should continue to have full faith in God, and in the Master. Generally, we only have faith when things go right, and the moment we experience some setback we start feeling Master is not competent, and we complain, "Master has not saved me from this!" We do not realize that the Master knows how we best can pass through our karmas. It is significant that the Masters say that during periods of poverty, ill health or ignominy, the greatest amount of our karmas are washed off. Our faith in the Master serves as a sheet anchor during difficult periods, and saves us from the mental torture and depression that may come to us during times of tribulation.

Surrender is a supreme state. It is not merely being resigned to whatever is happening. Being resigned to a situation means that we realize something is going wrong, but we learn to accept and live with it. Being surrendered means that we are so lost in our Beloved that we do not have any idea that something is going wrong! It is a much higher stage.

If we follow the path of surrender, we are no longer the doer; it is then the Master who is the doer in our life. Because he is aware of all the pitfalls of the path, once he becomes the doer all our problems are solved. Our problems become the Master's. Problems are always in respect to the one who is the doer. If the Master becomes the doer, the problems are his. Then we do not have to carry any burden; our Master carries all the burden for us. But we are strange passengers on life's journey. On this path, it is as though we are traveling in an airplane to our ultimate destination, and the Master is prepared to take on the burden of all our luggage. But while traveling in this airplane, we continue to keep our baggage and bedding on our own head! When the Master initiates us, he gives us an opportunity to cast aside our burden. He says he himself will take care of it. But we do not take advantage of what the Master is offering us. While sitting in the plane, we still insist on carrying our heavy baggage on our own head.

There are two paths on the spiritual way: the path of effort and grace, and the path of surrender. Most of us follow the path of effort and grace. Master's grace gives us the inspiration to make the first effort. His grace forms the first small arc, and then our resultant effort attracts a little greater dose of grace, which in turn forms another arc. Gradually, Master's grace and our consequent effort continue forming small arcs until the circle is complete. This is a path of struggle; sometimes we progress, and at other times we slip back. We climb two steps, and then slip down, and then start climbing up again. Sometimes our meditations are fruitful and sometimes they are not. Sometimes we are inspired, and sometimes we are bewildered and in the doldrums.

Only a lucky few follow the path of self-surrender. It is a difficult path, but if we are able to surrender, our life's journey becomes smooth and spontaneous. But generally we first try hard to make progress by our own efforts, and only after breaking our shins do we come to the stage of self-surrender. Ultimately, to reach our final goal we will have to surrender. There is no way out—sooner or later we all must come to that stage. It is just a question of whether we take a long time or come to it straight away.

If we succeed in surrendering ourself completely to the Master, then the spiritual path becomes simple, and we bypass many a circuitous route. Under the Master's guidance we travel by the shortest route. We reach our destination in the shortest possible time, and in the safest possible way. There is then no question of any skidding on the path, or of slipping into reverse gear. Once we have surrendered, we have won the game of love. We become the Beloved's, and the Beloved becomes ours.

PART IV

QUESTIONS
AND
ANSWERS

CHAPTER THIRTY
NEED
FOR A
LIVING MASTER

Question: Can we see God?

The Master: Yes, we can see God in this very lifetime.

Question: What is the proof of what you are saying?

The Master: Just as the proof of the pudding is in the eating, the proof of spiritual attainment is in its experience. We can attain self-knowledge and God-realization through mystic experiences on the path of the Masters. Once Ramakrishna Paramahansa was asked by his disciple Vivekananda, "Father, have you seen God?" He replied, "Yes, my son, I have seen Him as clearly as I see you."

When God came into expression He assumed two forms: the Light of God and the Music of the Spheres. It is by coming in contact with these two Principles that we cannot only see God, but we can talk to Him face to face, get His guidance in all our affairs, and ultimately merge in Him.

Question: What does God look like?

The Master: God is formless. He is all effulgence, all

Light, and pristine glory. God is so effulgent that we cannot describe His Light in detail, but it has been said in the scriptures that even trillions of suns and moons put together cannot vie with even one hair of God. We can see God in His pristine glory in the highest spiritual stage. But since the highest spiritual realm is beyond the reach of the mind and intellect mere words cannot describe it. It is said that in that stage we speak without tongue, we see without eyes, we hear without ears, we walk without feet, and we work without hands. All that has been said by the saints and seers about that realm is only a hazy approximation and a symbolic representation. But one thing can be said: There is no language there except for one, and that is the language of love.

Question: Where can we see God?

The Master: God has been seen by all saints and seers since the dawn of eternity. Guru Nanak has said, "I see my Lord before me." Other saints and seers have told us that they have seen God within. God has not been seen in the various places of pilgrimage because God does not reside in temples made by human hands; He resides in a temple which He has made Himself— that is, the human body. And the human body is the real temple in which we can see God in all His effulgence.

Question: Why do we need a living Master?

The Master: A living Master is one who has not only learned to die while living, and thus attained communion with the Almighty, but he is one who can teach others the technique of rising above body-consciousness so they too can attain the merger of their soul with God. Sincere seekers after truth go to a perfect Master to learn the above technique and reach their ultimate goal of self-knowledge and God-realization.

Question: Can a human being become one with God without the help of a living Master?

The Master: No. Simple and pure, a big no. N—O— both capital.

Question: How does a seeker know a Master is a true Master? What are the criteria by which we can judge who a Master is?

The Master: First, there should be a sincere prayer coming from the core of your soul, from the core of your heart, that the Almighty lead you to a perfect Master. Then, when you go to a Master and sit in his company it is a precondition that you should go with an open mind. Then you can make a list of all your questions, and see whether those questions are answered by the Master. When you sit in his presence you will experience a state of intoxication, a state of ecstasy, a state of peace, bliss and tranquility. That is the first criterion. The second is that if you follow the path as explained by him, he will give you a contact with the Light of God and the Music of the Spheres. This is a path of seeing, of firsthand experience. It is all a matter of practical experience, and of the radiation we get in his presence. A real Master is one who gives you this experience on the day of initiation. The extent of our progress and the extent of our experience may differ. Somebody may see the radiant form of the Master on the very first day; someone else may see the stars or different colors of Light. Similarly, one may hear the ringing of bells or the conch; and someone else may hear the sound of the cricket. The experience may differ, but each person must have an experience. Ultimately, that is *the* principle you can adopt in distinguishing a true Master from the so-called Masters.

The attributes of a perfect Master are fully described in the book *Godman*, by Sant Kirpal Singh. A seeker can, by applying the criteria given there, identify a Master. He cannot, however, judge the Master's true greatness because we can know a Master only to the extent he chooses to reveal himself. How can a disciple, who is like a humble man standing outside the portico of a palace, decide the greatness of an emperor?

Question: Are both seeing the Light of God and hearing the Celestial Music necessary for believing in the path of the Masters?

The Master: Yes, certainly. Spirituality is a science, and it is the most perfect science. Just as in science everything can be proved, so in spirituality, also, everything can be experienced and proved. We do not believe in blind faith. One saint has gone to the extent of saying, "Unless I have seen with my own eyes, I will not believe even what my Master says."

Question: So, if a person can get an experience of the Light and Sound of God from a teacher, can he take that teacher to be a perfect Master?

The Master: If a Master gives you the experience, then you can follow him. But it is only when you traverse the inner path that you realize the Master's true glory. There are very few Masters who give you this experience. The world generally has only one such Master at a time. There have been Masters who were contemporaries, but such occasions are few and far between. For example, Kabir Sahib and Guru Nanak were contemporaries.

Question: If a seeker has been initiated by someone who is not a true Master, and then leaves that particular Master, will he still be bound to that so-called Master, or can he go and take initiation from a true Master?

The Master: If you find that you have been initiated by a perfect Master, if you find that he has given you a direct contact with the Light of God and the Music of the Spheres, if you find that he has instilled love and compassion within you, and you are gradually evolving these qualities and are attaining more and more of Godhood, then you are blessed and should continue on the same path. But in case you find that you have neither been given contact with the Light of God and the Music of the Spheres, nor are you imbibing more and more love and compassion for mankind, then my advice to you would be to speak to your Master. Tell him that these are the attributes which you have to imbibe so that you may shake off the shackles of mind, matter and illusion, rise above body-consciousness, and ultimately have communion with the Almighty. Ask him to grant you these boons. If he is able to grant them to you, you are blessed and should continue following that path. But if, even upon your request, he is not able to help you, then you should go to a true adept who can grant you these boons. Let me give you an illustration. When we go to a professor and have to perform an experiment, we work honestly and diligently according to his instructions. If we perform the experiment in his presence and find that we are not getting the desired results, we should repeat it. But if, after our honest efforts, we fail again and again, and our professor cannot help us, then we have the right to look for another instructor. Similarly, in spirituality, we can go to another adept, but before doing so we must first go to our own teacher and make sure we have followed his instructions properly and completely. We should work with all devotion, with all zeal, and with all passion. Our faith should not falter or waver if we have failed once. But if we fail time and again, then it is best not to lose this golden opportunity of human life.

Question: Why do we need a Master who is living?

The Master: You always need a living Master. If a Master who has left this world could continue to guide you, what was the necessity of God sending so many saints throughout history? The first prophet that He sent after the creation of the world should have been sufficient! But God has sent thousands of saints and prophets since the dawn of eternity.

There have also been thousands of scriptures, but we have historical records of only a few. Even then, we have a record of so many saints, of so many prophets, and the wonder is that everybody says that their prophet was the last. If you believe that your prophet can guide humanity for all time to come, then why couldn't the first prophet sent by God do it?

From the beginning of time God has continued sending prophets and saints; why should He suddenly stop at a particular point in history? That is why Sant Kirpal Singh laid so much emphasis on the comparative study of religion. If we study the history of all saints and religions we find that the institutional side of religions, which came into being after the living Master or teacher left the earth, claimed their prophet or teacher to be the last. The Muslims say that Mohammed is the last of the Prophets. The Christians say Jesus was the only son of God. These views have created dissensions, crusades, religious wars, strife, hatred and inhuman atrocities, resulting in bloodshed all over the world. If we turn the pages of history we find how many crusades have been fought, how much blood was shed as a result of the fanatical attitude of people in all religions. In order to raise one mosque, one church, or one temple of bricks, people have razed to the ground thousands of *true* temples of God—thousands of human beings.

Some people believe that past saints and prophets are protecting them for all time to come. But Jesus has himself said in the holy Bible, "So long as I am in the world, I am the Light of the world." (John 9:5). The God Power, Christ Power, or Master Power has existed in the universe from the dawn of time and will continue to exist till the end of eternity. But it has been changing poles.

We respect and revere all saints. If we make a comparative study of religion we come to the conclusion that all saints irrespective of religion, caste, or color are sons of God. And if all saints are sons of the same universal Father, then where is the place for fanaticism, where is the place for forced conversions, where is the place for hatred, ego and vanity?

God has always sent Masters to this world, and He will continue to do so for all time to come.

Question: Since a spiritual Master comes from the highest region and has become one with God, does he live and function here on a different dimension than the rest of mankind?

The Master: No, he works at the same dimension as man. That is the beauty of the path. The Godman comes into this world, assumes the human form, and works at the same dimension as we do. If we are sitting on a high pedestal and talking to somebody who is sitting on the floor, whatever we might say about God, about separation from Him, about His glances and about His other lyrical qualities, the man who is sitting on the floor will always think, "Oh, he is sitting on a high pedestal, whatever he says is all right for him, but that is not applicable to me." The wonder of wonders is that the Godman comes down from his pedestal and sits with us at the same dimension we are sitting. He lives for nine months in the mother's womb, takes his birth, roams about as a child among children, as a youth among young people, calls somebody "Mummy," somebody "Auntie," calls us his brothers and sisters and addresses us as his "dear ones." He talks with us, he eats with us, he works with us, and sometimes he even jokes with us to establish that homogenity. Unless that homogenity is established, we do not get a confirmation in our heart of hearts that we can also do what he has done.

So after establishing a congenial atmosphere and helping us feel that we are working at the same dimension, he then talks about God and about the spiritual path. He talks about rising above body-consciousness, about dying daily while living. He speaks as if he is one of us and instills in us inspiration and assurance that whatever he has done we can also do. He then raises us from our worldly level by slowly elevating us and taking us with him on higher and higher planes. On the day of initiation he puts us in direct touch with the Light of God and the Music of the Spheres. He teaches us how to die while living, and helps us rise above body-consciousness and traverse the stars, the moon and the sun until we meet the inner radiant form of the Master. It is only then that we can begin to realize the Master's greatness.

In this connection, I am reminded of a story from the life of Peter the Great, the Czar of Russia. Once he went to Holland to learn the art of shipbuilding, and he assumed the form of an ordinary laborer. He found that many people from his own land had been banished to Holland. He felt sympathy for them, and wanted to bring them back to their home. He lived amongst them and gradually learned the art of shipbuilding. When he asked his countrymen why they did not return to their own country, they told him, "We want to go back to our country, but we are the cursed ones, the punished ones, the banished ones, and if we go to our country no one will accept us. If we enter our own country, people might scorn us and punish us." Peter told them, "Don't worry. I know some high officials there. I have come from Russia and I can intercede on your behalf. I can tell them how patriotic you are at heart, how you want to go to your own country and serve your own people. It may be that my intercession will change their hearts." Some of the laborers did not believe Peter. They thought, "He is just a laborer like ourselves." But others said, "He seems to be an honest man. He has rendered selfless service, he is full of humility and has given us guidance and help. Let us go with him." Those lucky few who accompanied him saw that when they passed the borders and entered the territory of Russia, people started saluting Peter. The laborers talked amongst themselves saying, "He may not be a top dignitary, but at least he is somebody who is known to these people."

As they proceeded towards the capital they found that even the high officials were paying their obeisance to him and were saluting him. Ultimately Peter led them to the highest court, sat on the throne himself and told them they were all welcome to stay in Russia. When the men asked, "Why didn't you tell us earlier that you were the king of Russia?" Peter said, "Had I told you before, you would not have believed me."

Similarly, God comes Himself in the human form to lead sincere seekers back to their true Home. The God Power, the Christ Power, the Master Power functions at all times, only the human poles change. Sometimes it is at the pole of Buddha, sometimes it is at the pole of Jesus, sometimes it is at the pole of Sawan or Kirpal. The Masters continually come from the highest spiritual regions to live with us here. They share our sorrows and joys, and live as one of us. Those fortunate ones who recognize and follow them rise above body-consciousness, traverse the higher planes and ultimately return to their true Homeland.

Question: Do the Masters have to be in the same spiritual line of succession?

The Master: No, they don't have to be in the same

line of Masters. The line may go from one religion to another, from one country to another. But there must be some line, because each Master has to be initiated by a living Master.

Question: Do you mean that if Kabir came back he would have to be initiated?

The Master: Yes. Some of the Masters receive a direct commission from God, such as Kabir and Soami Ji. But when they come into this world, they always go through the tradition of receiving initiation from a Master. For example, Kabir adopted Ramanand as his teacher.

Question: Even Jesus was baptized by John.

The Master: Yes, the saints maintain the traditions and the institutions, and they honor the system established.

Question: If we can see the Master in our meditation, what is the need for having the physical presence of the Master?

The Master: Having contact with the physical Master has its own charms and beauty. Whenever our Master, Sant Kirpal Singh Ji, would remember and talk about his great Master Baba Sawan Singh Ji, tears would come to his eyes. All Masters have said that the inner beauty of the Master is very attractive, very captivating, very enticing, but the outer beauty of the Master has its own special charm and upliftment.

Hazur Baba Sawan Singh Ji's talks were interspersed with humorous tales from our old scriptures. And during the satsang, he would laugh very heartily and make others laugh, and that was a regular feature of his discourses. But when the month of December

came, the month in which his own Master, Baba Jaimal
Singh Ji, left the earthly plane, he would be quite sad.
And on December 29, which marks the anniversary of
the final leaving of Baba Jaimal Singh Ji, he was so
moved that tears would flow from his eyes and
sometimes he would not be able to utter a word. So all
the saints, seers and mystics have longed for, sought
after and praised the physical form of the Master.

Question: What should a disciple do after his Master
leaves the earth plane, in order to find the Master's true
successor?

The Master: First, you should sit in meditation and
if you are lucky enough to see your Master within, then
you should ask him who his successor is. If you can do
this, then you can find out directly. Next, if you read
the book *Godman*, Sant Kirpal Singh Ji has very
beautifully described the outer signs of a saint. You can
always go with all humility to anyone who is said to be
the successor and find out whether those outer signs are
there. If you are sincere and receptive, you will
sometimes find the new Master physically changing into
your own Master, and the form will change back and
forth. Of course, you should always repeat the Five
Charged Names given by your Master to make sure that
what you are seeing, outside or within, is real, and not a
trick of the mind.

We should always remember that our Master is that
magnanimous personality who gives us initiation, and
we have to contemplate on his form even if he leaves the
physical body. When a Master leaves the physical plane
he continues to be in charge of the souls he has initiated,
and meets them the moment they come up to the astral

plane. But all duties which pertain to the physical form of the Master have to be discharged by his successor: giving guidance at the human level, replying to letters and queries, etc. This has been made amply clear in one of the letters written by Hazur Baba Sawan Singh Ji to one of his disciples in the United States:

> *Your question as to whom to look to for guidance if the present Master goes out of life is very appropriate. The Master leaves the physical frame in time like other people, but remains with his devotees in the astral form as long as the devotee has not crossed the astral plane. All internal guidance will be done by him, and it is he who will come to take charge of the soul at the time of death. And in the case where a devotee rises above the eye-focus now and meets him daily, he will meet him inwardly there as usual. He will continue to discharge his inward duties of guidance as before, but he cannot give instructions outwardly for the simple reason that he has left the physical vehicle. The functions which could be performed through the physical frame only, will now be done by his successor; all outward guidance will be done by his successor, and the devotees of the Master who is gone will love the successor no less. They will get the benefit of the outward instructions from the successor. Correspondence will be done with the successor, and you will know who it is.*

Even if the disciples' karmas have to be taken on by the Master on the physical level, that has to be performed by his successor. The moment the disciple goes beyond the nine doors and reaches the astral plane, then the radiant form of his own Master meets him and guides him through the higher regions. The Master may also bring the successor with him on the inner planes. So this is a basic principle. Because the successor has become one with your Master you can receive spiritual charging in his presence. But the true successor will not bind you to himself; he will bind you to your own Master. And he will always remind you that the Master who initiated you is your Master.

CHAPTER THIRTY-ONE
INITIATION

Question: Does the Master have to personally give the initiation instructions?

The Master: One can be initiated even if the Master is physically in one place and the disciple is in another. It is through radiation, it is through the charging that the newly initiated ones receive the experience of Light and Sound within. If the Master himself can initiate you in his physical presence, it is well and good. But if that is not possible because a seeker is far away, the Master may authorize someone to read out the instructions on his behalf. The God Power will function whether the Master is physically in the same place as the disciple or not, and people get the experience wherever they are.

Question: What does it mean that the Master can initiate just through his glance?

The Master: Initiation is attention. The "formal initiation" is a formality. There is a small anecdote from the life of the great Hazur which is relevant. Once Hazur was traveling by an express train, "The Frontier Mail." Coming from the opposite direction was a man riding a camel. Their eyes met, and the man on the camel said, "Oh, what godly beauty." That is all that happened. Now you can very well imagine for how much time the two eyes would have met. One is coming on a camel's back, and the other is traveling in a train which is going at forty miles per hour. But when, many years later, the man's time of death came, the man called one of his friends, who happened to be an initiate of Hazur, and said, "Your Guru has appeared within to take me with him!"

When Hazur completed his earthly sojourn and I went to Beas, the Beloved Master Sant Kirpal Singh sent me to find out how many people had been initiated. I checked and then told him that about 125,000 people had been initiated according to the record. But the Master said, "What about the countless people who had been initiated through his glances!" Initiation is through thought transference. It is all a matter of attention. Sometimes a single glance is sufficient.

Question: I am thinking of applying for initiation. What are the requirements?

The Master: All scriptures tell us we must lead an ethical life, which is a preparation for spirituality. An ethical life means a life of truth, love for all, chastity, humility, selfless service, and nonviolence. We must earn an honest livelihood and not be dependent on others. Another requirement is the maintenance of a strict vegetarian diet: abstinence from meat, fish, fowl, and eggs, both fertile and infertile. We must also avoid all alcoholic drinks and intoxicating drugs.

Before applying for initiation, you should search your soul and find out whether you are truly in a position to adhere to the prerequisites that have been laid down for initiation. If not, then please wait. Do not be in a hurry, because this is a commitment which you are undertaking for life. You should not come for initiation because of the influence of someone else. And you should not take initiation under pressure. So please give it much thought. If you are sincere, and fully prepared to adhere to the prerequisites, you are most welcome to apply. If you have any doubts, you are at liberty to discuss them with me. But apply for initiation only after all intellectual doubts have been removed and you are convinced of the validity of the path you are going to follow. Anyone who practices the path truly, honestly, constantly and accurately can be assured that he will have the desired results.

There is no difference between you and me. It is just that I had the good fortune of sitting at the feet of two great Masters, and was able to learn a little of their teachings. What one person has done another can do. This is a path of hope, of perfect hope. It is a path of experience, of realization, and not a path of feelings, emotions and inferences.

Question: I can understand the requirements for vegetarianism and leading an ethical life, but why are there restrictions on drinking liquor and taking intoxicating drugs?

The Master: To follow this path you must understand certain basic principles. First, we are of the same essence as God Almighty. God is an Ocean of All-consciousness, and we being of the same essence as that of God are also a conscious entity. Our soul is now lying in a dormant state. It is covered by sheaths of mind, matter and illusion. In order to take up the spiritual path we have to become more conscious. Spirituality is an awakening of the divine consciousness which is within everyone. We have to shake off these shackles and free our soul from these covers of illusion so that our soul regains its full consciousness and returns to God. If we drink alcoholic beverages, or use narcotics or hallucinogenic drugs, instead of expanding our consciousness we make it more dull and coarse. These things make our consciousness morbid, and we are not in full control of ourselves. You can become drunk by drinking from the glass, but to become drunk by drinking from the God-intoxicating eyes of the Master is something of which you are not aware. I have learned to drink from the lyrical glances of my Master, but that drinking makes me superconscious. It is diametrically opposite to what your liquor or drugs do—they dull much of the consciousness of the soul. Spirituality is a path of freedom, but if we become addicted to alcohol and drugs, then where is our freedom? Anything which is habit forming, or anything which dulls our consciousness, stands in our way of attaining the ultimate goal of our lives which is to liberate our soul from the clutches of mind and matter.

Question: What does it cost to follow this path?

The Master: Spirituality, like all other gifts of nature, is bestowed free of charge to seekers after truth. A true Master always earns his own livelihood and lives off his own earnings. He never accepts offerings or money from his disciples.

Question: How old do you have to be to get initiated into the Light and Sound?

The Master: Generally it is sixteen years old, but there may be exceptions. It all depends on how keen you are about getting initiated and how pure your soul is. The Master is the best judge. If you have a real zeal and passion for spirituality, then you can even be initiated at an earlier age. The Master will sometimes initiate a child, while an older person may be asked to wait for initiation. Age is not really a criterion. The criterion is the purity of the soul. Then again, children as young as five years old have been initiated into the practice of the Sound Current, and full initiation is given when the child is older.

Question: Does one have to give up his religion to follow the path of Sant Mat?

The Master: No, Sant Mat is a scientific path. It does not interfere with religions, rites or rituals. Everyone is told to remain in his own religion. But we tell whoever comes that if you are a Christian, be a true Christian; if you are a Jew, be a true Jew; if you are a Sikh, be a true Sikh; if you are a Muslim, be a true Muslim; and if you are a Hindu, be a true Hindu. Being a true follower of your religion means that you see the Light of God and hear the Music of the Spheres. We do not deal with the exoteric side of religion which pertains to outer forms of worship such as rites and rituals; we deal only with the esoteric side which is universal, which is concerned with firsthand spiritual experience.

We believe in the religion of humanity, in raising one's character and upholding the spiritual values. Sant Kirpal Singh used to say, "It is difficult to become a man, but once we become men in the true sense of the word, then it is not so difficult to find God."

CHAPTER THIRTY-TWO
DEATH
AND
KARMA

Question: What happens to the soul at the time of death?

The Master: This question can be divided into two parts: One part is the procedure relating to those souls who have been initiated and who are directly under the benevolent protection of the Master. It also applies to the souls who have fallen within the ambit of the Master because they had the good fortune to receive his glance of grace or attention, or because their near and dear relations are initiated by the Master. These souls fall into one category, and for them the death process which other souls have to undergo is not applicable. The other part pertains to those souls who have not been initiated, or who have not come under the protection of a perfect Master.

When our allotted time is over, the spirit currents withdraw from the body. First they withdraw from the toes. They then rise to the knees, then to the kundalini center, the navel, the heart, the throat, the tongue, and finally to the eyes. At that point the pupils of the eyes turn upwards and then come down, and the soul currents ebb out from their center in the body. Finally, the silver cord, which connects the physical body and the soul, breaks, and the process of death is complete. For those who are uninitiated, when their sensory currents withdraw they experience pain. It seems that every limb is twisting, turning and breaking. It is a painful process for several reasons. First, those who have not had the experience of withdrawing from the body during life are not used to that process. Then, we are so attached to our body that the moment we feel we are losing it we experience pain. If we are attached to our child, and we find the child is leaving us, how do we feel? Just imagine the plight of a mother whose child is snatched from her breast when she is feeding him. How would the mother feel? If we are attached to our parents, our spouse, or other relations, and we find we are losing them, we experience a big jolt. So, in the case of our body, when one part breaks, or is deadened, we not only feel the physical pain, but also mental and psychological pain. And this withdrawal is not a fast process either—the soul has to withdraw not only from one part, but from the entire body. It is a prolonged period of restlessness and anguish.

For those souls who are initiated, the Master Power enables them to pass through the whole process smoothly. In the case of a disciple, the Master is so gracious that the soul is able to withdraw in a very peaceful manner. Those souls who are initiated receive, from within, a forewarning from their Master of their impending death sometimes months in advance, sometimes weeks in advance, sometimes days or hours in advance. They can then begin preparing themselves for this final change. The soul passes through the inner stars, moon and sun, and beyond that to the radiant form of the Master. The Master decides to which inner plane the soul should be taken. If the disciple has been soaring high in meditation during his life, the soul at least goes to the plane it has reached. But if the soul has not been able to withdraw from the body during the disciple's lifetime, then it is for the Master to decide whether to place the soul on the inner planes or send the soul back for another human birth. Masters take the entire picture into account and give the maximum possible benefit to the soul. They usually place the souls on the inner planes. The soul remains there and meditates, and in due course the Master takes the soul to higher and higher stages, according to the soul's progress, until it reaches its Eternal Home. Finally, after passing through the higher stages, the soul attains ultimate communion with God. This is how the Master takes care of a disciple. For the initiate, death is a moment of peace, a moment of bliss, a moment of ecstasy. Kabir Sahib has said, "The death of which this world is afraid is a source of bliss for me, because it is only through this process of dying that I get eternal ecstasy."

Question: Why don't initiates experience pain at the time of death?

The Master: One reason is that those who are under the guidance of the Master learn from him the art of withdrawing the sensory currents from the body while they are still living. That helps at the last moment because it has been a daily feature in life. Take this simple example: When I was a young man I was regularly practicing both physical exercises and yoga asanas. The Beloved Master himself had mastered these in his youth and I learned them under his guidance in those early days. My body was so flexible, it appeared as if it were made of rubber or foam and could be twisted in any way, or bent in any direction. If I had never practiced these exercises, and had attempted to perform them all on a single day, I would have had pain in my muscles for about a week. Since I practiced them regularly, there was no pain. Similarly, if we regularly withdraw from our body, then it becomes a simple and natural process for us. If we have done it hundreds of times in life, then doing it at the time of death will not be any different. But even if initiates have fallen short of the mark and have not been able to rise above body-consciousness during their life, at the time of death the Master appears and helps them undergo this process smoothly.

Question: The Masters say that the time of death is fixed. Is it possible that the Master can change this date? And if so, for what reason does he do it?

The Master: Man comes from God with a capital of a certain number of breaths. He does not come with the commandment that he live for so many years and days. Those who indulge in pranayama, who stop their breath and sit in meditation, might have a longer life with the same number of breaths than those who dissipate their energies in certain labors or in the passion and panting of the sex act. The hour is not fixed, but the number of breaths allotted to man is fixed, and that is usually not changed. But the Master can prolong your life if he thinks that your existence in the world contributes to a noble cause. I have seen cases in which the Master has given a new lease on life to people.

Question: Are all our thoughts, words and deeds recorded?

The Master: Yes. Religions express this idea in many ways. According to the belief of the Muslims, for instance, there are two angels who are always recording what we do. It is said that they sit on our shoulders. The angel sitting on our right shoulder records whatever good deeds we do, and the angel sitting on our left shoulder records whatever evil deeds we do.

Question: How does the Angel of Death actually judge each soul?

The Master: The Angel of Death goes through the accounts to decide whether our good deeds have an edge over our bad deeds, and if so he commands that the soul be elevated to paradise which is a place of temporary bliss; it is not a place of eternal bliss according to the Path of the Masters of Sant Mat.

If the Angel of Death finds that there is a preponderance of evil deeds, then he ordains that the soul be sentenced to hell. In hell there are various tortures—tortures of fire, of intense hunger and unquenchable thirst, and many others. The soul remains in either heaven or hell for a length of time which is determined by the preponderance of good deeds over evil deeds, or evil deeds over good deeds. If one has a much greater degree of bad deeds than good ones, his stay in hell will be longer than that of someone whose bad deeds are only slightly greater than the amount of good deeds. But if both the good deeds and evil deeds balance out, then the soul is placed in what the Sufis call *ahraf*, an area intervening between heaven and hell. When the period of stay in either heaven, hell, or ahraf is over, the soul returns for another birth in the 8.4 million species of life. In the case of those who have come to the feet of a living Master, at the time of initiation the record of good and bad deeds is immediately transferred from the custody of Dharam Raj to the Master. It is then the Master, not the Angel of Death, who meets the soul within at the time of death. The Master ensures that even if a disciple must come back for another birth to finish his spiritual journey, he will not go below the human body.

Question: Is hell a specific region or a condition of one's own mind?

The Master: It is a specific region.

Question: What are the different ways people suffer in hell?

The Master: According to the *Shrimat Bhagavat Purana*, an ancient Hindu scripture, first there is a stream of blood and pus that souls have to pass through. Actually, such descriptions are symbolic as words cannot really depict the tortures. But the scriptures do give some descriptions. They say that you have such great thirst there that if you had an entire ocean to drink, your thirst would not be quenched; but despite having such a great thirst you do not get a drop of water to drink. Parts of hell have extreme cold and one feels a greater chill than you would feel at the North Pole. There is also continuous hunger and intense heat. There are such fires in hell that one has the sensation of being burned all the time, and you cannot escape. Some of these descriptions resemble those found in Dante's *Inferno*.

Question: When the soul or consciousness is in hell, does it know the reason for its suffering there?

The Master: Yes.

Question: Does the pain leave some impression within so that the next time the soul is in the human form and is confronted again with the same temptations it will remember the terrible pain it has suffered as a penalty for that sin, and avoid it?

The Master: The illusion is so great that as soon as that period of torture is finished and the soul gets another life, it forgets all about its experience in hell. That is the worst part of it—you are made to undergo this pain, but you are not allowed to benefit by it. If you retained the consciousness that you had undergone so much pain and torture, you would never again do anything wrong. The purpose of the Negative Power, the lord of the three worlds, is to make such great labyrinths for the soul that once it gets out of one labyrinth it goes into another. He does not want to lose any souls in his domain. It is written in the scriptures that when the child is in the mother's womb, it suffers a lot. The child hangs upside down, and its body and bones are formed in intense heat. It then prays to God, and the soul cries out: "When I am born, I will spend all my life in Your devotion, in Your service, in Your meditation." It makes a sincere promise so that the Almighty will release it from the mother's womb. But the moment the child comes into the world, the illusion is so great that it forgets all about its promise. The soul forgets the experiences it underwent with the Angel of

Death. But if the soul were even to remember its promise made in the mother's womb, it would not do anything wrong after coming into this world.

Question: Does the soul have a form on the astral and causal planes?

The Master: On the astral plane you have the astral body, and on the causal plane you have the causal body. These forms get more and more radiant and rarified as the soul progresses through the inner regions.

Question: Sant Kirpal Singh said that it is very important to meditate while on earth because you make much more progress here than you do in your meditation while on the inner planes. Could you explain this?

The Master: That is true; you do make much quicker progress on earth. If we put in time for the meditation practices in this physical life, our progress on the spiritual path is much greater than if we put in the same effort when we are placed on some inner plane after death. This is actually one of the reasons our Master sometimes decides to give us another human birth.

Question: What do souls do on the inner planes?

The Master: They have all the time at their disposal to pray and meditate. Even in this world what do the true lovers do? One of my verses is: "I have no friend except the Beloved, and I have no vocation except His love." If this is the disciple's condition in this world, then what else is there to occupy him on the inner regions? All we have to do is be devoted to Him, have love for Him and meditate on Him.

Question: What happens to the consciousness of the soul of a person who is senile?

The Master: The soul never becomes unconscious. It is the brain which becomes senile. The difficulty is that when we are in the human body, our soul, our body and our intellect are so intermixed that we are not able to distinguish one from the other. But the soul is always a conscious entity.

Question: If a person is senile or if he is in a vegetable state, is there a means of communicating from soul to soul to give him comfort?

The Master: Yes, an evolved soul can give comfort because he is a fully conscious being, and always communicates from soul to soul.

Question: Would you speak about abortion and when the soul enters the body?

The Master: The soul enters the body at the moment of conception, and from that time on, the child which is being formed is a conscious entity. Abortion is considered to be one of the most heinous crimes that anyone can commit. Normally people resort to murder, butchery and assassination only when they have life-long enmity, or when they have been oppressed and downtrodden by oppressors who have played havoc with them. They resort to assassination or killing their fellow beings because they have been victims of acts which fill them with hatred, animosity and ill will for a long time. The other case when people resort to murder is when they are excited beyond control, when somebody exploits them, somebody plays with their self-respect, somebody plays havoc with something they consider dearer to them than their own life. Killings are also a result of national frenzy, when we go to war to pursue national or political interests, or to uphold national honor. We seldom come across cases where people resort to the cold-blooded murder of the innocent, of those they have not even seen, of those who have not done us any harm, of those who bear us no ill will, no hatred. But in the case of an abortion we are guilty of such a heinous crime. The child does not have any hatred for us; he does not have any ill will for us. The child has not done us any harm. Yet, we are prepared to perpetrate the cold-blooded murder of this symbol of innocence. By any civilized standard, murder of an innocent child in the make who does not even have the ability to do anything wrong, is the most cruel and inhuman act that can be committed.

Question: Is there anything we as initiates can do to give comfort when we know that a person is dying?

The Master: When an initiate is dying, all should sit in meditation. We can always pray to our Master. Even if the dying person is not initiated, we can still pray to the Master for the soul's peace and spiritual welfare.

Question: Is it right for a disciple to ask the Master for relief from physical ailments?

The Master: In the initial stages of discipleship, whenever the slightest thing goes wrong in the office or in business, if there is some acute or prolonged physical ailment, the disciple prays to the Master. If the disciple does not ask everything of his Master, then from whom should he ask a favor? And if the disciple is a pampered one or a delicate and sensitive person, he will ask the Master to heal him of even a pinprick. In the initial stages of discipleship there is nothing wrong in doing this. It shows that the disciple is looking to only one source, bowing his head in obeisance to only one, and that is his Master. The trouble arises when we bow at every threshold, seeking relief for our problems. If we go to somebody who uses occult or healing powers and then go to a shrine, and then go to the Master, we are bowing at every threshold.

What is permissible in the early stages of discipleship, however, becomes a sacrilege in the higher stages. As the disciple progresses, he rises above body-consciousness, becomes one with the Master and traverses the higher planes. At that stage, he is supposed to act on the principle, "Sweet is Thy will." Then, any request to the Master goes against this principle, and for an advanced disciple it becomes a sacrilege. If we act on the principle, "Sweet is Thy will," where is the question of asking for the curtailment or for the short-circuiting of physical ailments?

Question: Is it a result of our karmas that we commit certain sins or that we indulge in bad habits?

The Master: Too much emphasis can be laid on karma. People use karma as an excuse to hide their own weaknesses. By attributing their bad actions to the law of karma, they think they have a justification for continuing their negative pattern of life. A poet once said, "Even if a leaf rustles, it rustles by the will of God. You say that man is sinful. I don't understand; if the rustling of a leaf on a tree is ordained by God, then my becoming a sinner is also ordained by God." People indulge in adultery and say, "God has ordained that. Unless God has ordained this adultery how could I commit it?" This attitude is nothing but a wile of the mind. Our tricky mind is a thousand-headed cobra which will try to prevent us from traversing the path of righteousness. The mind will always present some excuse or the other to make us lead an immoral life. It will come forward with all sorts of excuses, pleas and arguments in favor of leading a sinful life. But if we have decided to make the goal of our life self-knowledge and God-realization, then we need to exercise firmness and curb these arguments put forth by our mind so we can follow the right path.

Question: Are problems that arise in a marriage mainly the result of our past karmas or are they a result of our actions in the area of our free will?

The Master: Problems in marriage are due to both, but are mainly due to our own ego. I find that many of the troubles in married life are the result of each partner thinking that he or she is the superior one. If we are able to overcome our ego, develop right understanding and lead a harmonious life, then we can be successful in our worldly affairs as well as our spiritual affairs. We should try to be humble. We should try to rid ourselves of our ego, because it is our biggest stumbling block. Whatever we say or do should be in a loving manner; a congenial household atmosphere will help greatly in achieving our spiritual objective.

CHAPTER THIRTY-THREE
POSITIVE MYSTICISM

Question: In order to follow the path of the Masters, do we have to leave our family, our job, or our worldly life?

The Master: No, we do not have to leave the world and go into the mountains or the jungles to find God. The path of Sant Mat is not a path of negative mysticism; it is a path of positive mysticism. Mysticism has two approaches: the negative and the positive. The negative approach of mysticism teaches us to leave the world, our family, our hearth and home, our jobs, and our everyday routine. It teaches that we should be unconcerned with the world, and go to the icy caves of the Himalayas or to the thatched huts of the desert and spend all our time in meditation and penance. That is negative mysticism, of which the Masters of Sant Mat do not approve. The Masters believe in the positive approach of mysticism, in which we live in the world, become useful members of society and discharge all our obligations and duties, but in a spirit of detachment. We have to maintain our home, earn our livelihood, support our family, bring up our children properly, and serve our elders. We have to be good citizens of our state, our nation, the world, and ultimately we have to be good cosmic citizens, because our duties which start in the narrow limits of our family have to be expanded to the level of the cosmos.

Positive mysticism means we must earn our own livelihood, stand on our own legs, and share with others. Those who follow the path of negative mysticism and become ascetics depend on other people for their meals. It is a basic concept of mysticism that if you depend on others for your sustenance, you have to surrender a portion of the benefits of your own meditation to the person who feeds and supports you. You are no longer independent. Guru Nanak has said that it is only those who earn their livelihood by the sweat of their brow who can truly follow the path of mysticism. So we should attend to our occupation or business, and perform our duties honestly in that field.

In whatever line we work, we should strive to complete our assignments or conduct our business in a perfect manner. On the path of positive mysticism, excellence is the key word. Whatever we do in life, we should do well. Yet, while doing our best, we should not be attached to the results. This means that after performing our duties, we should stop thinking about them and do our meditation with single-minded attention. The key to success in any sphere of life is to work with one-pointed attention. Those people who carry their office to their home, and who carry their home to their office, do not achieve success in life. Outstanding success is achieved only by those who work with one-pointed concentration. When such people are in the home or in their office they attend to their duties and are very useful in that sphere. But the moment they attend to their meditation they do so with single-minded attention, forgetting everything else. When they attend to their Master's work, they accord it the top priority, and during that time they concentrate only on that work.

Guru Nanak has said that we should be like the lotus flower which stays in the water and is yet unaffected by it. Or we should be like the swan who swims in water, but whenever it wants, it flies with dry wings. In the same way we should attend to all our responsibilities, but should perform them in a spirit of detachment so we can rise above this materialistic tangle whenever we want.

Question: The Masters say that someone who practices meditation learns to die daily, and even hundreds of times a day. How is it possible to do this and still carry out all our worldly duties?

The Master: This refers to the technique of dying while living. The scriptures say, "Learn to die so that you may begin to live." Once we learn this art, we can practice it every day, ten times a day or even a hundred times a day. Hazur Baba Sawan Singh used to tell us that there is a stage when our soul's condition is such that it can fly at will from the human body to the Creator, and then come back to the body in the twinkling of an eye. When our soul traverses the inner planes and then comes back, the journey does not tire or exhaust the soul, rather the soul gets rejuvenated. It is blessed with renewed vigor, renewed zeal, renewed passion. When it returns to the body it is bubbling with life, and we can better attend to our duties in the world.

Question: Is selfless service possible, and if so, how can we develop this quality?

The Master: We learn by example. But if we look around we find that in all spheres of our life selfless service is conspicuous by its absence. Our friends and relations and those on whom we rely fail us badly when it comes to the question of selfless service. When we are affluent and circumstances around us are good, everybody comes to us, everybody tries to befriend us, everybody talks about his relationship with us. But if unfortunately we fall into evil days in matters of health, finance or reputation, then see what happens. All those who claimed they would give their lives for us, start considering us untouchables. They avoid us so they might not be implicated with our suffering and our ill luck. This is the way of the world.

Of all the human relations the one between the mother and the child is the greatest example of selfless service. Yet even in that relationship a mother expects something in return from the child as the child grows up. But the supreme relationship in this world is that of a Master and a disciple. The Master selflessly gives, gives and gives in all spheres. We can imbibe the quality of selfless service from someone who is an embodiment of that quality. And that person is a saint.

Question: How can the relationship between a husband and a wife be a helping factor on the spiritual path?

The Master: Marriage is a sacrament, not a contract. The scriptures tell us that marriage means taking a companion in life, in weal and woe, to help each other to know God, which is the highest aim before us in the human body. We need a companion in life. Whomsoever God has united, let God alone disunite. It is the unseen hand of God that brings two souls together to wind up the give and take of reactions from the past. It is not a coincidence but something preordained, a divine dispensation that comes about at the appointed time.

The Masters have stressed the importance of leading our married lives in a sublime manner to ensure a happy earthly sojourn. The basic principle to be followed for a successful companionship is the principle of humility coupled with a honeyed tongue. This lays a strong foundation on which the marital edifice is raised and generates mutual trust, confidence and reverence. And if both partners have a harmonious life, then they become like two wheels of a chariot, running smoothly and leading them to their destination. If husband and wife help each other on the spiritual path, they will be able to attain the ultimate goal of communion with God in a much shorter period than normal.

While marriage is no bar to spirituality, we do have to observe a certain discipline, just as we have to for success in any other sphere. We must lead our spiritual life according to the tenets of the scriptures which prescribe that sex be used only for the purpose of procreation. Marriage should not be used as a license for indulging in sensual pleasures. Our physical body is not meant to be an instrument for sensual gratification. The physical enjoyments are only transitory. What we are looking for is eternal enjoyment, eternal happiness, eternal bliss.

Sant Kirpal Singh stressed that marriage has a deep inner spiritual significance. He emphasized the importance of righteous living, coupled with sweet remembrance of God. Such a disciplined life can help us develop inner longing to meet and merge with God.

The need for creating a harmonious and happy married life is more acutely felt in our present-day society which supports and even advocates divorce for one reason or another. There is an acute problem, especially in the West, of what is called incompatability between life-partners. But this can be overcome by sincere and loving efforts. Human beings are, after all, subject to error. If we can learn to forgive and forget, most of the hatred and anger will vanish, and that will bring in more peace and love. If one of the marriage partners has any bad habit, it can be washed away with the water of love. Tolerance and patience result in mutual reverence. Acceptance of each other's legitimate demands inevitably helps to develop resignation to the will of God, because it is God in each of the partners who is to be revered and loved. We should remember that the physical bodies of the life-partners are two separate entities, and the soul is the only unitive factor.

Question: I understand that your father, Sant Kirpal Singh, gave you three pieces of advice when you got married. Would you tell us what they were?

The Master: The first thing that he told us was that we should try to adjust to each other and cover each other's weaknesses. He said that happiness is another name for adjustment. He advised that neither of us should stand on our false prestige, but at every opportunity should try to adjust to each other's point of view. That advice has helped us the most in making a happy life.

The second thing he told us was if little differences of opinion arise, we should sit together in a spirit of cooperation and understanding and reconcile them ourselves. We should not complain to others about them. He said we should never go to sleep at night without having first reconciled our differences.

Besides this, he explained the basic tenets of chastity according to our scriptures and the teachings of the saints, and how we should lead our life in a pure manner. His advice has enabled us to have a very congenial atmosphere in the house.

Question: Why do so many newly married couples argue with each other so much?

The Master: If we review the early years of a marriage, we find that most of us are foolish because we fight over trifles. We make these trifles points of prestige and try to prove ourselves superior to our partner. This results in many unnecessary arguments and miserable moments. Much of the misery caused in the earlier years of a marriage is due to the partners' lack of understanding of each other. Unfortunately in the West, disagreements caused by eccentricities, idiosyncrasies and trifles are taken to be points of prestige, and because people are unwilling to adjust, there are many divorces. When people know that they have to remain together they learn to adjust; their eccentricities are gradually pruned, their idiosyncrasies are gradually curbed, and the two wheels of the chariot start moving much more harmoniously.

In India, traditionally, there is no question of

divorce and remarriage. The moment this realization comes into the minds of a married couple, they make adjustments. And we do that in so many spheres of our lives. In the office we may have a boss who is very eccentric, who is very rash, but somehow or the other we make adjustments. In business we come across officials or important customers who are difficult to deal with, and again we make adjustments. We adjust to people and circumstances that are not to our liking. But in one of the most important and sacred spheres of our life, marriage, we feel that there is no need to make adjustments. Marriage is a sacrament, not a contract. You can cancel a contract, but no man has the power to cancel a sacrament. Unfortunately we do not realize the sacred nature of marriage. We think it is like going to the market to purchase a mango. We taste it, and if it is sweet, we eat it, otherwise we throw it away and select another one.

Once we realize that we have to adjust to our life-partner, these troubles will not arise.

Question: Most theories of psychology and philosophy say that man's urge for sex is a natural impulse, just as hunger is a natural impulse. The world is full of all sorts of theories that sexual activity is normal and typical of man. Can you tell us what is expected of a healthy, pure man, and how he should relate to a woman?

The Master: Psychology and other sciences deal only with the mind and emotions; they do not deal with the soul. Love is innate in the soul, but lust is not innate. We acquire lust through the impressions we receive. The theory of impressions is that whatever you see, whatever you talk about, whatever you hear, whatever you perceive through the senses goes from the conscious to the subconscious mind. From the subconscious it goes to the unconscious. Then from the unconscious it unpredictably comes back to your conscious mind. And after some time it becomes a habit and in due course habit becomes your nature.

Jesus said, "Blessed are the pure in heart for they shall see God." When we have a sincere heartfelt desire to be pure and chaste we automatically develop chaste thoughts, and these chaste thoughts help keep us from the allurement of sex. This development of chastity is a natural and spontaneous process born out of our zeal to follow the spiritual path.

The scriptures teach us that a husband and wife should engage in sex only when they want children. It is said that from the moment a woman conceives until the child is weaned from the breast she and her husband should lead a completely chaste life. It is said that to lead a pure life, men should consider women who are older than them as their mothers, those their age as sisters, and those younger than them as daughters. Similarly, women should consider men who are older than them as their fathers, those their age as brothers, and those younger than them as sons.

Question: We want to have a child. Is there anything we can do so that we can have a very spiritual child?

The Master: If parents want to have a spiritual child, both the husband and wife should be leading a chaste life. Then, when they want to have such a child, they should do so when both are praying to the Lord for that blessing. It should be during those sanctified moments, when both are thinking of the Lord. Then it is a pious moment. If the mother conceives at that time, the child will have saintly tendencies. But if the husband and wife are in a fit of passion when conception takes place, then the child will be affected.

Question: What can we do if we want our children to follow the spiritual life we lead?

The Master: If we are following the spiritual path and are regularly devoting time to our meditation, if we are living our lives according to the teachings of the Masters, then naturally our children will ask us, "What are you doing? Why are you doing it? What are you aiming for?" We can tell the children that we are trying to meet God during our lifetime through the process of meditation as taught by our Master.

If we develop the higher human values, treat our children with love, affection and consideration, and are really ardent and keen about the path, they will have faith in our way of life and believe in us. Children in this era are very wide-awake. Children today are much more aware than we were at their age—they are very perceptive. If they are satisfied that we are leading an ideal life, they will surely be affected and will try to follow in our footsteps.

Question: How can I have more tolerance for the behavior of my children?

The Master: Love is the panacea for all these problems. It is the duty of the parents to bring up the children in the best possible way. For this, they have to be patient. They have to put up with the eccentricities of their children, with the odd behavior of their children. Children are, after all, children. If parents deal with them with love, tolerance and patience, the children will improve.

One important way we can help ourselves in this regard is to sit in meditation each morning. If we do this, then during the day these little things will not upset us. We will be peaceful and able to withstand little inconveniences.

Question: What can we do to help our children in school?

The Master: Parents should teach their children to respect their teachers. And similarly, the teachers should teach their students to respect their parents. When I was a child, when we were at home we were asked to respect our teachers, and when we were at school our teachers asked us to respect our parents. We were shuttling back and forth from the teachers to the parents and from the parents to the teachers, and each emphasized that we respect the other. Naturally we inculcated a lot of respect for both. But now, unfortunately, this is not happening.

Parents should also devote time to their children. If the children are learning to read, the parents should help them. Children who are properly encouraged at home keep pace with their schoolwork and excel. If parents and teachers take a real interest in the children, then the children will put in their best effort. I do not believe that children should be shackled or enchained, but at the same time they should know what they have to do. We should see that our children learn to strive for excellence at school. They should not be content with mediocrity. We should see that they also become good citizens of the world. So, raising children capable of spiritual and intellectual achievement, with good characters, and able to grow up to earn an honest and comfortable livelihood is the parents' obligation.

Question: How can we inculcate discipline in our children?

The Master: If parents give their children love and attention, it will have a great impact, a very beneficial effect on the children. "Charity begins at home," and if the parents devote time to their children it will have a healthy influence on the children.

Some parents feel that their children should be free to do as they please. They themselves do not want to lead disciplined lives; they want to have their own freedom. But if the parents do not want to be bound by discipline, then their children will also want their full freedom. And then, when the children exercise their freedom and thrust their fists in the face of their mother and father, the parents cry and complain. If you demand the freedom to walk in the middle of the road, then motorists will surely demand the freedom to run you down. And to some extent that has been the pattern of modern life.

Fortunately, today many people are harking back to their hearths and homes. The life-style based on freedom from both discipline and responsibility is losing its appeal. There is a growing movement to develop a deeper sense of commitment to our families, our relations, our communities. And if we ourselves begin to lead more responsible, disciplined lives, then our children will naturally inculcate those qualities.

Question: Why should we respect our parents?

The Master: To answer this, I will give you a

practical example. Take an earthenware pitcher, fill it with sand, tie a rope to the head of the pitcher and tie the other end to your belly. Go around the whole night wearing this pitcher and then you will have an inkling of what your mother has done for you. Your mother carried you, she carried that pitcher of sand for nine months. And we ask, "Why should we respect our parents?" Your mother fed you from her own blood, and she turned that pitcher of sand into an oasis. You were created from her own body: your veins, your respiratory tract, your digestive tract, your hands, your feet, your ears and your eyes. If you are able to see and hear, it is because of your mother's care, because of her prayers. She was the medium through which God gave you the gift of life. And while being that medium she had to suffer. We do not undergo an iota of what our mother has suffered for us. This reason alone is sufficient to elicit our profound gratitude to her for the rest of our life.

It is true that some parents do not sacrifice as much as others, and after the child is born many parents continue their club life and leave their children to the care of babysitters. But during those nine months, there were many times when she sacrificed her social life. Do you sacrifice your social life for your parents for even one day?

Your father also sacrificed so much for your sake. While bringing you up, your needs became priority number one, and your mother's needs were relegated to priority number two and your father's needs became priority number three. And your father had to work for years to pay for your food, your clothes, your medical expenses, and your schooling.

Of all worldly relations, parents are our best well-wishers. It may be that they wish you to follow their pattern of life, their pattern of thinking, but that desire is born out of their good wishes for you. They may get annoyed, they may punish you, but it is only out of their good intentions.

Have you ever taken so much interest in anyone else? Have you ever given of yourself so much? And what do they do it for? They do it as selfless service.

Question: Our parents come to visit our home, and they are meat eaters. Since we are strict vegetarians, would it be disrespectful if we did not serve them meat?

The Master: I have been working with people who were in the habit of drinking liquor and eating meat, but when they visited my home, I did not serve them those things. I did not think it right to purchase with my earnings anything that was prohibited by the spiritual teachings. On the days your parents visit, you can lovingly serve them the vegetarian dishes.

Question: Do you feel it is always the woman's responsibility to look after the child or could it be a shared duty with the husband? It does not seem fair that the woman always has to miss her meditation time or miss attending satsang in order to care for the child, while the man is able to go to satsang and put in time for meditation.

The Master: If both husband and wife happen to be on the spiritual path, then the natural attempt is to help each other progress spiritually. It is a herculean job to raise a child, and it consumes much time. If the husband tries to help the wife by taking on a little responsibility himself and sharing the burden with the wife, then both can benefit from satsang and meditation, and there will be smooth sailing. According to the circumstances you have to arrive at an acceptable formula for sharing responsibility. It is only by cooperation, ungrudging cooperation, that you can progress on the path. Willing cooperation is the keynote.

Question: Is it sensible to have a modest savings to provide for our retirement or to provide for our child's education?

The Master: Yes, we have to. If we have children, then it is our duty to give them a good education to prepare them for their own tasks in life. And we also have to make some provision for a rainy day. We will require some savings or some pension which will provide for us after retirement.

Question: What profession is most suitable to take up?

The Master: Ours is a path which does not require us to renounce the world and go into the mountains or jungles. We have to live in the world, but while doing that we should avoid any job that causes us to do something which is unethical and not in accordance with the spiritual path we are following. If we can find a profession in which we can help mankind and serve those in need, we are most fortunate and should adopt it.

There are a number of noble professions; for example, the medical, the agricultural and the teaching professions. Both the medical and educational professions help in man-making, and anything that helps in man-making is noble. When practicing in these fields we should be imbued with a deep sense of service. Material gain should not be our main goal. At the end of the day we should have the satisfaction that we have helped others. If you want to go into business, then you should first gain a complete knowledge of it. You should know what the pitfalls are. To gain experience and knowledge you can start out by working for a company in that field. Then, if you wanted to, you could start your own business. But whatever business you take up, one thing I would like to emphasize is that we should not do anything which is unethical or violates the human values. We should try to do good wherever we are; whether we are in a helping profession or in our own business. We should always be honest and fair. If we fall victim to temptation and use some underhanded means to raise our profits or to harm our competitors, then that will count against us. But if we are able to compete in a field, with all honesty and in accordance with the rules of the game, then we will not lose anything on this path.

Question: I am working in a position where everybody caters to the needs of their important customers, clients or superiors. Everybody caters to their demands to win contracts or to get their work done. It is expected that I entertain them with meat and alcoholic beverages. Is this all right?

The Master: This question was asked time and again to our great Master, Hazur Baba Sawan Singh Ji, and then to the Beloved Master, Sant Kirpal Singh Ji. And the two great Masters replied very strongly by saying, ''What I do not take myself, what right have I to offer it to others?'' Just look at the way our mind tries to trick us. If we were to follow your way of thinking we would get derailed from the ethical path. Once we begin to abandon our principles it is very difficult to apply the brakes. So long as we are steadfastly following the path, our voice of conscience will be loud, and will warn us the first time we slip up. But if we do not listen to that voice and we deviate further, the voice of conscience will grow weaker and weaker. And after a few transgressions it almost disappears.

People in various spheres of life, in government, business, law, and in almost all the professions have asked the same question—whether it is necessary for us to be scrupulous in entertaining others, even if we ourselves avoid taking meat and wine, even if we ourselves avoid doing those things that are against our principles. On this point the Masters have been extraordinarily firm. If we are on the spiritual path we must not only abstain from these things ourselves but it is as necessary that we do not pay for or arrange for others to do those things that violate our principles.

Question: In my job as an administrator, how can I keep the people I supervise happy and also make them work?

The Master: If we are the supervisor or boss in an office, we should be very benevolent. The latest management theories say we should take a more human approach to dealing with people. We should try to understand the difficulties of our subordinates and then help them to the extent possible. We should always be willing to extend a helping hand. The art of administration is the art of bringing out the best in people.

If we instill a feeling in them that there is somebody above them who is very considerate, very concerned about them, then we will be able to win their hearts. If this type of relationship between an administrator and his subordinates develops, then we will find that working conditions will be congenial and harmonious. The subordinates will feel quite at home and it will give them a lot of psychological anchorage and happiness.

When I was an administrator and I had workers who did not do their job, I kept them under my personal supervision. I was a hard taskmaster. I made them sit in my own room and work, even those who were notorious for not working. I have not yet come across anyone who is not amenable to love. While I was firm, I was also most loving. I tried to help my subordinates and co-workers to the maximum extent, and the result was that they started respecting me. If they start respecting you, then good and honest work will come as a by-product.

Once there was a man who had received bad reports for seven continuous years. His promotion and his increment had been stopped. Ultimately he was sent to me to work in my section and I was to report on him after seeing his work for three months. After I gave him a good report the director of administration called me and asked, "Do you know the man you are recommending, and do you know about his record?" I said that I did, and he went on to ask, "Do you mean to say that ours is a charitable institution and not a government office?" I said, "Sir, charity begins at home, and I believe that every office should be charitable to the staff so that we can get the best work out of people."

He then asked, "What do you mean? How is it that you have given a good report to this man? Do you mean to say that you are better than the seven people under whom he worked previously?" I said, "I do not claim that *I* am a better man, but I do claim that *he* has certainly become a better man. There is a complete metamorphosis in him. My only request is that you transfer him to your own office and keep him under your personal observation for a period of time, and then decide for yourself. I am sure you will find him so changed that you will want to retain him on your own staff." He smiled and signed the papers, and the man's increments were given to him.

Question: I try to avoid people who lead me astray and cause me to violate my principles. But sometimes I find myself criticizing them.

The Master: Avoiding situations is not criticizing the situations, or criticizing the company; it is just following your path and sticking to your principles. Suppose I am ill and the doctor has advised me to adopt a special diet and avoid certain foods and activities. The people around me may be taking foods or doing things which are forbidden to me, but my avoidance of those things does not mean that I am criticizing them. Similarly, if we adopt a way of life in which we avoid those things which hinder our spiritual progress, it does not involve criticism of those who are not following our way of life.

Swami Ram Tirtha said, "Wanted, reformers: not of others, but of themselves." The tendency to criticize others is born out of our thinking that it is our birthright to reform others. We criticize others when we start feeling that we are superior to them. But on our path we have only to look to our own selves, to reform our own selves.

Question: I am sometimes criticized because of my diet and beliefs, and because I keep aloof from people who are always talking about sex in a very explicit manner. Sometimes I argue about this with others, but that does not seem to help. What should I do?

The Master: If you really follow the path of the Masters, other people will automatically begin to respect your feelings and your way of thinking. This has been my experience in life—but it takes some time. To start with they may say that you are an introvert, that you are unsocial. You may be dubbed with many of these unpleasant labels. But if you are loving, and stick to your principles, then other people will begin respecting your views. Ultimately, some of those who were your critics may even begin to adopt your way of life.

I was a government officer for about twenty-five years, and I was a member of the officers' club. At lunchtime many of my fellow officers met together and they talked about films, about nightclubs, about sex, about crime, and other worldly things. I was always most cordial and friendly, but I would only meet them for lunch once a month, and that was with the understanding that on that particular day they would not talk about such things. And with the grace of the two great Masters, some of them eventually came to the feet of the Masters.

Our trouble arises when we are not true to ourselves, when we put on a camouflage, when we behave differently in different situations. If we are uniform in our way of life, then, after some time, people start respecting us. No amount of arguing or intellectual wrangling will help us. It is only by our example that we can win their hearts.

Question: Sant Kirpal Singh talked of minding our own business. Does that conflict with the need to develop compassion?

The Master: Minding our own business means that we put in the requisite number of hours in our meditation, we lead an ethical life, and we engage in self-introspection every day. Minding our own business means that we do not take it upon ourselves to reform others and lecture them, "You should be more ethical," or "You should do your meditations," or "You should donate one-tenth of your earnings." We should try to reform ourselves first, and while doing so we must be compassionate. Compassion is a part of leading an ethical life. Minding our own business does not mean that we cease to have love and compassion for others. If someone is in difficulty and undergoing deep sorrow, or having physical or financial troubles and is caught in the mire of mind and matter, it is our duty to help him to the extent we can.

Question: If we are to be humble on the path, does that mean we should be passive?

The Master: There is a difference between humility and passivity. Humility is a gift that is granted to our heart, to our soul, and it is reflected in our words and in our behavior. Humility is the negation of ego and egotism. It means that we do not harbor ideas of superiority or snobbishness. It means that we are aware of our own weaknesses, and do not look to the weaknesses of others.

Being passive is the opposite of being active, and unless we are active, unless we are full of zeal and passion, we will not be able to progress on the spiritual path. If we are passive we idle away our time in inaction, like the opium-eaters. Ours is a long and difficult journey. We must be active; we must develop the desire to attain our goal if we wish to get the maximum benefit from the precious moments of this short life with which we have been blessed.

Question: I find that I am able to stay inspired to pursue the spiritual path when I am around spiritually-minded people. But when I am around people who are very negative or only interested in worldly pleasures, I become affected and slip from the spiritual path. What can I do?

The Master: One thing we can do is avoid spending too much time with those people who lead us into all sorts of temptations, brawls, quarrels, exchanges of hot words and having unchaste and negative thoughts. Especially in the initial stages we are on a very delicate footing. We should have love for all, and should not have bad thoughts about those people, but it is better to avoid unnecessary association with those who cause us to fall prey to these weaknesses. Instead we can adopt the company of those who inspire us to greater efforts on the spiritual path and instill in us love for the Master and for all creation. When we have advanced sufficiently on the path and are strong enough to withstand any disturbances, then we will not be affected, even by those people who have negative tendencies. Those who make progress on the spiritual path, who listen to the higher strains of the Music of the Spheres and see the higher manifestations of the Light of God within, are not affected by others. They radiate love, compassion, purity and humility. And whoever comes within the radiation of such people, even someone who is full of negative traits, is gradually changed. They are able to convert the ape in man to the angel in man.

So if we ourselves are in a vulnerable position, we have to avoid the strong negative influence of others. But if we progress spiritually and are in a position to influence others and change them from the negative to the positive path, then we can safely associate with them.

CHAPTER THIRTY-FOUR
LOVE
AND
DEVOTION

Question: Could you talk about the relationship of love and sacrifice on the spiritual path?

The Master: God is love. Our soul, being of the same essence as that of God, is also love. And the way back to God is through love. The path of the Masters is the path of love, and if we look at history from the dawn of time, we will find that the path of love has been the path of sacrifice.

If we want to understand anything about this path we should look at Christ who was put on the Cross; at the great Sufi, Shamas Tabrez, who was flayed alive; at Mansur who, for crying out *Anal-haq* (I am God), was sent to the gallows. Again, we can look at the example of Guru Arjan Dev who was made to sit on a hot iron plate beneath which fierce fires were burning, and to add to his torture, red hot sand was poured on his body. When Hazrat Mian Mir, another mystic of the time, saw this he could not bear it; he wanted permission from his friend, Guru Arjan Dev, to annihilate the Moghul oppressors and to raze their forts and courts to the ground. But the Guru replied, "Do you think that I cannot do that myself? Ours is the path of acceptance and surrender to the will of God." And he met his end chanting, "Sweet is Thy will."

We also find in the life of the tenth Guru, Guru Gobind Singh, that in defending the right of spiritual freedom he had to lose all his sons. Two of them were entombed alive within a wall which was built around and above them. The other two sons were slain in the battlefield. The great Guru said, "My four sons are gone; they were a sacred trust from God. If God has taken back His sacred trust, it is His own sweet will. I still have thousands of other sons who are my disciples in the name of God." So the path of love is one of self-less sacrifice. This is what the saints, seers and mystics have sung for ages.

Just imagine what is required of us when we start treading this path. A great Sufi poet has said, "I have given my life, I have given my heart, I have given my faith, and still I am happy and grateful to God that I have received love in return. This is a priceless bargain." So if a disciple can receive the lyrical glances of his Beloved Master, the love-laden glances of the divine Cupbearer, he will attain ineffable bliss. For such ecstasy, one's heart, one's life, one's faith are worth the sacrifice. This is a path which demands so much from us that very little is left. It is a path which gives us so much; there is no parallel to the gifts of the Master.

This is a path on which paradoxically the Guru does not demand anything from us; he gives spirituality to us as a free gift like all other gifts of nature. Yet at the same time, he does not leave anything with us. He takes everything away. He takes our heart, he takes our soul, he takes away all our attachments to the world. So this is a strange paradox: On the one hand we are told that spirituality is given as a free gift like all the other gifts of nature, such as water and sun; but on the other hand, when we experience the fruits of spirituality, when we become absorbed in the intoxication of the Master, we become totally oblivious to our own self and in that state of oblivion we are bereft of all that is worldly. Only that which is spiritual, only that which really belongs to us, remains.

Once we decide to take up this path, we should be prepared to pay its price, whatever it is. In this short span of our worldly life, we have to achieve so much. We have to rise above body-consciousness, we have to cross the inner stars, the inner moon and the inner sun. We have to come face to face with the radiant form of our Master within, and achieve our ultimate communion with the Creator.

A living Master is the greatest blessing on earth. He has solved the mystery of life and death and has become one with the Creator; he can help us in traversing the divine path so we too can become one with the Creator. It is only through the medium of a living Master that we can travel this path. This is why we seek protection from a living Master who gives us the gift of initiation at the most appropriate moment.

Question: The path of love seems so difficult, so full of tests. Why does the Master have to put us through these tests when he already knows everything about us?

The Master: The Master does not test us intentionally. There are regular difficulties on the path, and we misinterpret them to be tests. If we accept these conditions as normal features on the path, and we do not misconstrue them to be tests, then everything will be set in its proper perspective. They are not difficulties meant for you alone; everyone who traverses the path faces them. We should take something personally only when what we have to undergo is not to be undergone by others. It is our ego that makes us take a normal feature of the path to be something especially contrived against us, and we call it our test. When we call it a test we only magnify our own difficulties. The trials on the path are great, but they are not as severe as we make them. It is due to our misconceptions and misunderstandings that we have so much self-created pain and suffering. The path is a difficult one, but if we could see it in its true perspective then we would minimize the pain and traverse it happily. We must grasp two concepts. First, the storehouse of the Master's love is not depletable. His love is infinite, and always with us. Second, we have to be grateful for what we get and then crave for more. There is an Urdu verse which says:

> *This is a gift of God, O friend,*
> *It does not lie in the control of any*
> *human being.*
> *You should go on spreading the apron*
> *of your gratitude*
> *And continue asking for more and more.*

Question: Sometimes my faith is shaken when I go through the "dark night of the soul," when I feel God and the Master have abandoned me. I lose confidence that I will ever have the Master's love again.

The Master: Your faith must never be shaken. Once we have come to a Master, where is the question of losing faith? Remember he has taken a vow never to leave or forsake us until he takes us to our eternal Home. But we should also realize that we *must* go through the stage when we feel abandoned, when we feel that the Master has deserted us. This is one of the features of the path of mystic love. We must go through this stage without a grumble on our lips, for this stage is in reality a gift from the Master himself to help us grow. Ultimately, it is for our own benefit, for our own salvation. There is a divine purpose behind everything the Master does. We may have to spend a lifetime of tears to get his love. We cannot demand the gift supreme from our Beloved. The gift descends at the appointed hour. One of my verses says:

> *This secret has revealed itself to me:*
> *Love is not a dew drop, it is a spark*
> *of fire.*
> *Cast just one glance of grace on me and*
> *I am prepared to undergo sorrows*
> *for the whole of my life.*

Question: What can we do to receive more grace from the Master?

The Master: Patience and perseverance should be the keynotes of the life of a seeker after truth. Acting in divine wisdom, the Master grants us the object of our longing, the object of our pining, when the appropriate time arrives. So we have to be patient, and we need much perseverance on this path.

We should fulfill our duties to the best we can in our

own humble way, in a spirit of complete dedication, in a spirit of complete self-surrender. This is a path on which we have to shed our ego; we have to send egotism to the winds. This is a path on which we have to leave behind all impatience and impetuosity and wait for the divine will to have its way in the realization of our dreams, in the realization of the prime objective of our life. This is a path on which we have to surrender our will to the supreme will of God. We also have to realize that with all our creative powers, all our hard work, all our consistency, all our constancy, all our persistence, we are still not worthy of attracting the grace of God, of catching the eye of a saint who is Word-made-flesh. With all our attainments we not only fall short of the requirements, but we are very much below the minimum standards which a Master sets for traversing the path of spirituality.

When we are praying to the Lord while sitting in the presence of a saint we should never try to demand anything as a matter of right. We should always pray to God Almighty and to the Master to grant us the boon for which we are desirous, for which we long and pine, not as a matter of right, but as a matter of grace and compassion.

Dr. Muhammed Iqbal, a great modern Urdu poet who called himself a disciple of Maulana Rumi, says: "I know I am not worthy of your glance, but look at my passion, at my perseverance."

We can never claim as a right the lyrical, God-intoxicated glances of the Master. We can never claim as a matter of right that a perfect Master should elevate us so as to have union with the Almighty. The earlier we realize this basic principle, this fundamental tenet of the path of mysticism, the faster will be our progress. If we expect spiritual progress as a matter of right, it is an expression of the ego in us. Even in the arts, we find that musicians, poets, painters, sculptors, and dancers, reach the height of attainment only when they are blessed with inspiration. The greater their humility and devotion to their art, the greater their attainment.

Ultimately, it is humility, and the cry of our soul for compassion and grace, which are effective on the path of spirituality.

OTHER BOOKS

BY DARSHAN SINGH

The Secret of Secrets: Spiritual Talks
The Cry of the Soul: Mystic Poetry
The Challenge of Inner Space
The Meaning of Christ

BY KIRPAL SINGH

Godman: Finding a Spiritual Master
The Crown of Life: A Study in Yoga
Morning Talks
Naam or Word
Prayer: Its Nature and Technique
A Great Saint—Baba Jaimal Singh: His Life and Teachings
Jap Ji: The Message of Guru Nanak
Spiritual Elixir, Vols. I and II
The Teachings of Kirpal Singh (compiled and edited by Ruth Seader)
Vol. I: The Holy Path
Vol. II: Self-Introspection/Meditation
Vol. III: The New Life (complete in one book)
Heart to Heart Talks—Vols. I and II (edited by Malcolm Tillis)
The Night Is a Jungle and Other Discourses of Kirpal Singh
Man! Know Thyself
Spirituality: What It Is
The Mystery of Death
The Wheel of Life: The Law of Action and Reaction
A Brief Life Sketch of Hazur Baba Sawan Singh Ji Maharaj
God Power/Christ Power/Guru Power

BY OTHER AUTHORS

Portrait of Perfection: A Pictorial Biography of Kirpal Singh
The Beloved Master, edited by Bhadra Sena
Classics & Creations: A World of Vegetarian Cooking
The Ocean of Grace Divine, edited by Bhadra Sena
The Saint and His Master, by B.M. Sahai and R.K. Khanna
Seeing Is Above All: Sant Darshan Singh's First Indian Tour,
edited by H.C. Chadda
Kirpal Singh: The Story of a Saint
compiled and adapted for children; with illustrations

ORDERING BOOKS

Books listed on the preceding page may be ordered through your bookseller or directly from Sawan Kirpal Publications, Route 1, Box 24, Bowling Green, VA 22427, or Sawan Kirpal Publications, 2 Canal Road, Vijay Nagar, Delhi-110009, India.

SAT SANDESH: THE MESSAGE OF THE MASTERS

This monthly magazine is filled with practical and inspiring articles on all aspects of the mystic experience. Discourses by the living Master, Sant Darshan Singh, provide the initiate and seeker with information and guidance on meditation and the spiritual life. Also included are articles by Sant Kirpal Singh and Baba Sawan Singh. Poetry, photos, and other features appear in each issue. For subscription information write: Sat Sandesh, Subscription Dept., Route 1, Box 24, Bowling Green, VA 22427.

FURTHER INFORMATION

Mr. T.S. Khanna, General Representative, 8807 Lea Lane, Alexandria, VA 22309.

Olga Donenberg, Midwest Representative, 6007 N. Sheridan Rd., #14-B, Chicago, IL 60660.

Sunnie Cowen, Southern Representative, 3976 Belle Vista Dr. E., St. Petersburg Beach, FL 33706.

Sant Darshan Singh resides at Kirpal Ashram, 2 Canal Road, Vijay Nagar, Delhi-110009, India.